Where God Finds You *is emotionally capturing, yet accurately written. It allowed me to see the people of the Bible less as symbols or superheroes and more as real, broken, and ordinary people who needed God just as I do.*

—RACHAEL LAMPA, RECORDING ARTIST

A wonderful devotional, capturing the truth and poignancy of how biblical characters clearly speak to our busy, twenty-first-century lives.

—BILL MYERS, BEST-SELLING AUTHOR,
ELI AND *THE GOD HATER*

Anita Higman delivers on the promise of her subtitle, bringing the characters of the Bible alive with her deft retelling of biblical stories that have strong application to our twenty-first-century lives. This collection of devotions will bless you all year long.

—DEBORAH RANEY, AUTHOR,
A VOW TO CHERISH AND
THE HANOVER FALLS NOVELS SERIES

Anita Higman brings biblical stories to life. Sharing what Bible characters learned and how their lessons apply to each of us today, Where God Finds You *is a soul-impacting compilation.*

—KIM VOGEL SAWYER, BEST-SELLING AUTHOR,
MY HEART REMEMBERS

In Where God Finds You, *Anita Higman has brought biblical accounts to life in her creative, dramatic retelling. This fresh look at Bible stories is good for group study, in which readers can examine their attitudes and actions and grow in faith and submission to God, regardless of circumstances. Thought-provoking questions lead us into a deeper study of the Bible. Readers can experience what the author realized: "Jesus is nearer than I'd imagined and cares more than I'd hoped."*

—YVONNE LEHMAN, BEST-SELLING, AWARD-WINNING
AUTHOR, DIRECTOR OF THE BLUE RIDGE
"AUTUMN IN THE MOUNTAINS" NOVELIST RETREAT

ABOUT ANITA HIGMAN

Higman is an excellent writer who will captivate you and pull you into an unforgettable story.

—KIMBERLY BYRD

In Love Finds You in Humble, Texas, *Anita Higman has created a humorous, deeply felt love story that celebrates small-town life, sisterhood, and the power of love to heal the past.*

—SHARON DUNN, AUTHOR,
THE BARGAIN HUNTER MYSTERIES

Anita Higman always tells a good story, and I really enjoyed Love Finds You in Humble, Texas. *A tantalizing tale of love with endearing characters and believable conflict combined with a strong faith message.*

—BARBARA WARREN

MORE TITLES BY ANITA HIGMAN

Love Finds You in Humble, Texas
Love Finds You Under the Mistletoe (coauthored)
Another Grave Matter
Mom Matters
A Merry Little Christmas, October 2012 release
Texas Wildflowers, November 2012 release

Where God Finds You

40 DEVOTIONS BRINGING BIBLE CHARACTERS TO LIFE

ANITA HIGMAN

Award-Winning Author

Standard®
PUBLISHING

Cincinnati, Ohio

To my agent, Sandra Bishop, at MacGregor Literary.
Thanks for always going the extra mile for me—
for believing in my work, for the prayers and the cheers.
I appreciate it all.

Published by Standard Publishing, Cincinnati, Ohio
www.standardpub.com

Printed in: United States of America
Project editor: Laura Derico
Cover design: Claudine Mansour Design
Interior design: Dina Sorn at Ahaa! Design

In this book, the dialogue presented in the stories is generally quoted or carefully paraphrased from either the *New International Version* or the *King James Version* of the Bible. All other Scripture quotations, unless otherwise indicated, are taken from the *HOLY BIBLE, NEW INTERNATIONAL VERSION®. NIV®.* Copyright © 1973, 1978, 1984, 2011 by Biblica, Inc.™ Used by permission of Zondervan. All rights reserved.

ISBN 978-0-7847-3363-9

Library of Congress Cataloging-in-Publication Data

Higman, Anita.
   Where God finds you : 40 devotions bringing Bible characters to life / Anita Higman.
     p. cm.
   ISBN 978-0-7847-3363-9
1. Bible--Biography. I. Title.
   BS571.H44 2012
   242'.5--dc23

                              2012021204

17 16 15 14 13 12   1 2 3 4 5 6 7 8 9

For the word of God is alive and active.
HEBREWS 4:12

Oh! for a closer walk with God.
WILLIAM COWPER

Contents

A Letter from Anita

I talk to God.

I talk to God, because I desire to hear from him. Isn't that what we all crave—what we long for with every breath? To know the master of creation still cares about his clay figures—the ones he breathed life into. Us. You and me.

Some days, I can hear Jesus so clearly. He's saying, "I love you. I created you. And I haven't forgotten you. I am still here, even in the dark places. The lonely places. The places you can't share with anyone else but me. I'm listening.

"Talk to me."

Where God Finds You is my humble attempt to bring the ancient characters of the Bible into your living room. To give you the chance to see these men and women in the light of your daily routine. And to give you the opportunity to hear Jesus speaking through these lives in a slightly different way.

You'll see their issues, their messes, and their victories. And you'll notice how much they look like your own. You'll discover how God takes each person, then and now, and speaks into their moments the message of his love. And you'll witness the miracle of how we all can live out our lives with him by our side on this earth, until we're right where he wants us to be—with him in heaven.

Through reflection on Scripture and prayer, my hope is that you'll discover a place in each of these lives of vulnerability, tenderness, truth, and love—a place where you can find God . . . and where God finds you.

Anita Higman

ONE

The Woman Who Touched His Cloak

She thought, "If I just touch his clothes, I will be healed."

MARK 5:28

My name is Mara. I lived with a strange illness—one that had no cure. I bled for twelve years, and I was like the parched desert ground. There was no life left in me.

When I was a child, my life was filled with laughter. And at night I often dreamed of lilies. I would gather them from the fields and breathe in their fragrance. But as I grew older, my dreams faded. There were no lilies. Only the odor of sickness.

Year after year I gave all my wages to physicians, but my condition only worsened. They had remedies with frightening rituals—pits and chants and vines set ablaze. This malady drained my whole being while the doctors drained my purse!

My name, Mara, means "bitter." But I am not without hope.

One day I heard of a healer who would be coming to my village. He would be passing through that very day, so people said. Wrapping myself in my least tattered cloak, I made my way with hurried steps to the other side of a stone dwelling—hiding from the crowd that hastened by me. The people murmured about a man who was known for his stories and his touch. The man was a rabbi named Yeshua—Jesus.

The mob moved like a swarm of locusts around this man, Jesus. I caught only a glimpse of his face and saw his cloak swirl behind him as he disappeared in their midst.

I clutched my garment, twisting it in my cold fingers. Even within my hope, doubts gathered like vultures. What would he know of my loss of blood? I had heard reports that he was no more than a carpenter. And that he was from Nazareth. There was certainly no honor in his place of birth!

> *The people murmured about a man who was known for his stories and his touch. The man was a rabbi named Yeshua—Jesus.*

And yet he was hailed as a great prophet and teacher. And a healer. At last my desire for healing surpassed my fear. I stepped away from the shadows and out into the light.

And oh, such light that rained from the heavens that day. Or was it from . . . him? The radiant glow was so glorious, I covered my face with my veil.

I joined the tide of people, but their closeness made me unsteady on my feet. I could not get enough air. Dark whispers came to me. *You are cursed. Your ailment is from the very hand of Beelzebub.* The never-ending hiss of condemnation that had haunted me for years spoke poison into my mind.

With each step I faltered in my spirit. *I am unclean. My fine tunic is forever stained. I am the tares among the wheat. The broken pottery that is cast off. I am no better than the wild dogs.*

Who was I to approach this rabbi? I would only bring more shame to my family, and my touch would surely make Yeshua unclean. Would the crowd put me to death? I continued forward even amidst the twisting storms of fear and self-loathing. Voices swirled in my head like the rabbi's swirling cloak.

His cloak. The idea came to me—a small seed of faith. *I could just touch his cloak.* Perhaps it was a foolish notion—the desperation of a sick woman's mind. But I felt that if I could just reach the fringe of his cloak, I would be made whole.

Jesus walked very near me, but he did not face me in the crowd. Knowing my intentions, I shook with fear—my fingers felt like dry earth crumbling into pieces. I focused on his feet, and watched the edge of his robe dragging in the dust of the street. I hesitated for just a moment and then reached down, just brushing my fingertips on the edge of the dusty cloth.

A burst, like a flash of light in the night sky, struck my body and flooded me with warmth. And straightway the fountain of my misery dried up. I knew at that moment I had been released from my plague.

I wanted to stay near him—Jesus—for all eternity. Instead, I stumbled back, frightened, and the crowd swallowed me up. But I was no longer alone. I felt his presence still.

I heard a commotion among the people, and then I heard Jesus' strong, clear voice: "Who touched my clothes?"

His disciples replied, "You see the crowd pressing in around you. And yet you ask who touched you?"

His disciples did not understand him. But I understood. He knew of my touch. I saw Jesus—he kept looking around, seeking me out—the one who had done this thing. Trembling, I fell down before him and told him the whole truth.

Jesus said to me, "Daughter, your faith has healed you. Go in peace."

Daughter? Why would he address me so? I lifted my veil for just a moment, wanting to see him without my shroud. I wanted to know this rabbi who had done such a miracle.

Jesus was unlike any man I'd seen before. He was without fine features, and yet the angles of his face were noble and without flaw. His hands were clean, but rough. In his eyes—those dark, knowing eyes—were the deep sea and the color of ripe figs! They were full of thunder, and yet his upturned mouth put me at ease. I reflected on his countenance, feeling no shame.

This stranger—this rabbi—was no ordinary man. Surely he was the long awaited Messiah, as people had been saying!

On my journey home my step was light—my heart no longer troubled, but joy-filled. For the first time in many years, I knew that on this night, I would dream of lilies.

THE STORY FROM GOD'S WORD

MARK 5:24-34

A large crowd followed and pressed around him. And a woman was there who had been subject to bleeding for twelve years. She had suffered a great deal under the care of many doctors and had spent all she had, yet instead of getting better she grew worse. When she heard about Jesus, she came up behind him in the crowd and touched his cloak, because she thought, "If I just touch his clothes, I will be healed." Immediately her bleeding stopped and she felt in her body that she was freed from her suffering.

At once Jesus realized that power had gone out from him. He turned around in the crowd and asked, "Who touched my clothes?"

"You see the people crowding against you," his disciples answered, "and yet you can ask, 'Who touched me?'"

But Jesus kept looking around to see who had done it. Then the woman, knowing what had happened to her, came and fell at his feet and, trembling with fear, told him the whole truth. He said to her, "Daughter, your faith has healed you. Go in peace and be freed from your suffering."

THE STORY—FROM THEN TO NOW

When I think of the woman in this Bible story, I always wonder how embarrassed she was about her strange ailment. Shame and humiliation are common human emotions, and I admit I've had these feelings more times than I can count. Some of these unhappy life events were terribly painful. Some were my fault, some weren't. Some were ones I'd like to forget, and some might even be considered humorous.

Recently I ran a grocery cart over my toe at the store, and instead of letting out my emotion, I stopped, flinched, and groaned quietly. I must have looked like a lobster just dipped into a pot of boiling water. I was embarrassed at my clumsiness. Somehow it felt better to absorb a few seconds of pain than to shriek and see the disapproval or terror on the faces of the people around me. Funny thing about humans—we tend not to let people know we're injured. We turn the hurt inward.

> *No matter what century we live in, we all are subject to the tendency to run from God when there's trouble, instead of running into his arms.*

The woman in the story had much more to deal with than just everyday embarrassment. By Jewish law she was considered ceremonially unclean, which must have enhanced her feelings of shame. Also, she might have been in daily physical pain. After all the doctors failed, she could easily have turned her misery inward, pulling away from people and suffering in silence. She might have been close to giving up.

No matter what century we live in, we all are subject to the tendency to run from God when there's trouble, instead of running into his arms while we wait for an answer to our prayers.

In spite of all her suffering, this woman still had a seed of hope. She entered the crowd that day to seek out Jesus for his divine help. She exercised faith. And that faith made her whole.

Throughout this commentary I've never used the woman's name, because it was never mentioned in the Bible. Mara, the name I chose to use in the story, was fictional. However, even though her name was never revealed in the Scriptures, her great act of faith has continued to impress Christians for generations. And most of all, her faith pleased and impressed God.

✤ THE STORY ✤
QUESTIONS TO THINK ABOUT

1. Do you think the emotional pain Mara faced would have forced her into a solitary life? What would such a life be like?

2. After all the failures in her treatments, when she heard about Jesus coming, what do you think went through her mind? When you have gone through trials and disappointments, how has your hope been affected?

3. Why didn't she just ask Jesus to heal her as nearly everyone else did? Why do you think she chose to touch his cloak?

4. Why did the woman hide after she was healed? What reasons would she have had to fear?

5. If you had been healed of a terrible illness, what would be the first thing you would do?

6. Why do you think Jesus wanted to meet this woman after she was healed? Did you think Jesus was going to be angry at the woman?

7. So many times we assume God is angry with us when he really wants to be closer to us—to be involved in our daily lives. Have you had that experience in your life—when you ran from God because you thought he was unhappy with you? Talk about that time. What is a better response to God's love and mercy?

TWO

Joseph, Son of Jacob

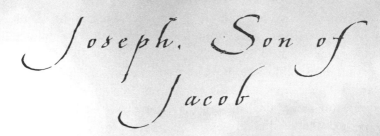

So when Joseph came to his brothers,
they stripped him of his robe—the ornate
robe he was wearing—and they took him
and threw him into the cistern.

GENESIS 37:23, 24

My dreams have blessed me, and my dreams have cursed me.

I rested my head against the rocky walls—my gloomy prison chamber—waiting for my death. Like the howling desert winds, in a fit of fury my brothers had swept me up and hurled me here. And where was here? This cistern must have a name, just as mine was Yosef. But unless I am rescued my name will be no more.

The mud clung to my skin, cooling my burning flesh. Yet I was uncertain if the dampness was from the ground or from the blood oozing from my wounds. I felt thirsty, but I had no water to drink. *If I had a vessel of your living water—oh, Lord! I would pour some of it out to you as an offering . . . for your kindness to me. But I would also beg for divine mercy, for your deliverance.*

I rose from the floor, and inch by inch, using the protruding stones in the wall as footholds, I hoisted myself upward. But I tumbled back down, this time wounding my arm. My might and courage failed me, and my spirit surrendered to this abandoned place. I was broken like this well. It no longer held water, and I no longer held hope.

I gazed upward, laboring to see the bits of shifting light above me. No women would draw water from this empty well, nor would my father hear my cries. He could not have imagined that his sons would carry out such an evil plot. My brothers, who once loved me, now call me "this dreamer," and have given me over to death. Even the brute beasts of the field do not leave their prey to writhe in agony. Even the jackals put their wounded out of their misery.

My brothers were now slaves to corruption, and yet my heart did not fill with hate. Perhaps my father's love for me produced resentment. Perhaps I spoke of his devotion too often. My father's gift to me may have been unendurable to them. My long cloak made of fine fabric was so ornamental and beautiful in every detail—fit for a prince. Everyone who saw it was filled with admiration and envy. But now it was gone—stripped off my back by my own blood.

> *I was broken like this well. It no longer held water, and I no longer held hope.*

I could not help being my father's beloved. And yet, were my father's boasts too discordant among my brothers, his affections too unjust?

Was I at fault, Lord, that I've been thrown into this strange underworld? The very dreams you gave me were in my heart and on my lips. Even the sheaves of grain and the sun and moon and stars bowed down to me. Was this not truth? Should I have remained silent?

The words of rebuke from my father echoed in my head, "What is this dream you had? Will your mother and I and your brothers actually come and bow down to the ground before you?" But yet he loved me still, and trusted me.

I wept for my foolishness, for my boastful words. I cried out in the darkness, "Oh, God, my God, I believed you were well pleased with me—that you had filled me with wisdom and prophecy. But was I full of falsehood and haughty pride? You know every part of me. Search my heart."

Then I wept for my father, who would lament over my death. All his joy would be slain. Again I wept and prayed. "My Lord, my mighty God, my Fortress, do not forsake me. Rescue me from this darkness, this earthen pit, and I will live the rest of my days for your sake. I will abandon my dreaming, my visions, if it be your will. I surrender to your sovereignty."

In this empty prison I felt a presence—Yahweh encircled me, bringing me hope and comfort.

In the midst of my supplications, I fell into a profound sleep. Then, some time later in the evening hours, I awakened to the sounds of rustling above me. And strange voices. "Oh, God, is this a dream too? Or is it my deliverance?"

THE STORY FROM GOD'S WORD
GENESIS 37:23-28

So when Joseph came to his brothers, they stripped him of his robe—the ornate robe he was wearing—and they took him and threw him into the cistern. The cistern was empty; there was no water in it.

As they sat down to eat their meal, they looked up and saw a caravan of Ishmaelites coming from Gilead. Their camels were loaded with spices, balm and myrrh, and they were on their way to take them down to Egypt.

Judah said to his brothers, "What will we gain if we kill our brother and cover up his blood? Come, let's sell him to the Ishmaelites and not lay our hands on him; after all, he is our brother, our own flesh and blood." His brothers agreed.

So when the Midianite merchants came by, his brothers pulled Joseph up out of the cistern and sold him for twenty shekels of silver to the Ishmaelites, who took him to Egypt.

THE STORY—FROM THEN TO NOW

Joseph's trauma has always intrigued me. It's impossible not to wonder what he was thinking and feeling down in that abandoned cistern. The horror of it, the desperate pleas for help, the clamoring, gasping attempts to escape from the pit. Or perhaps he felt regret, the guilt of past offenses. Perhaps a moment of surrender to the sovereignty of God.

Everyone, no matter how sheltered, will have plenty of those Joseph moments of earthly terror. Maybe not in a physical pit, but there will be enough travail to make us feel like we've been thrown into a dark abyss. I've had more of those encounters than I can count. Events that cornered me into impossible situations, so that all there was left to do was surrender my will to God's sovereign plan. Once I did that, my spirit stopped its struggle.

> *Have you had a moment like Joseph's—*
> *a moment of reckoning and surrender?*

We don't know from reading the Scriptures what Joseph was thinking in that cistern, but I can imagine there was more going on than merely being frightened in a dark place. We do know that Joseph loved his family enough to later deliver them from a terrible famine. He forgave them to the point that seeing them again moved him so deeply, he shed tears of joy.

Have you had a moment like Joseph's—a moment of reckoning and surrender? It's what we do with those moments that counts. It's easy to trust God in the basking-in-the-sunlight times, not so easy when we are tossed into a pit of trouble. But God has proven himself faithful, not only in the Old Testament, but in today's world—and in each and every life.

1. Why do you think Joseph didn't realize that he was filling his brothers with anger . . . until it was too late?

2. Today we often speak of dreams as being just a way our brain deals with experiences we've had or thoughts in our subconscious mind. From Joseph's story or other Bible stories, what can you tell about how people thought or felt about the importance of dreams?

3. Do you think Joseph had regrets about the way he talked about his dreams? Why or why not?

4. Have you ever been a part of a sibling rivalry? How did it make you feel? What kind of problems does favoritism cause within a family?

5. In this passage from Genesis 37, we find that Reuben wanted to save Joseph, and was apparently absent when his brother was sold to the Ishmaelites. This was just one of several times in Joseph's life when he could have been rescued from his trouble, but wasn't. But we're told in Genesis 39:23 that God was "with Joseph and gave him success in whatever he did." What do you think this tells us about God and his plans? What does it say about how we look at our successes and failures?

6. When Joseph, the dreamer, wasn't restored to his home but sold into slavery, what do you think he was feeling? Hatred? Revenge? Despair? Think of a time when you've been in a dark place emotionally or spiritually. How did you feel? What did you want to say to God?

7. What helps you remember that God is with you, even in the darkest places?

THREE

Mary, Mother of Jesus

But the angel said to her, "Do not be afraid, Mary; you have found favor with God."
LUKE 1:30

looked up from the spindle as a mystifying radiance spun its way into the room. It came into my presence like the falling of olive blossoms in the breeze, white and gleaming. Awestruck, I watched as the light took on the form of a creature of light!

I rose quickly, my heart bolting like that of a newborn lamb. I moved away from the light until my back pressed against the mud-brick wall. A faint sound, like a lyre, could be heard, as if music radiated from his snowy robe. His face shone. Could it have been the lingering glow from being near the throne of the Almighty?

"Greetings," the angel said. "You who are highly favored! The Lord is with you."

I wanted to speak but could not. With tremulous hands I fingered my veil but did not lower it. What could this mean? What kind of greeting was this?

This being spoke again. "Do not be afraid, Mary; you have found favor with God. You will conceive and give birth to a son, and you are to call him Jesus. He will be great and will be called the Son of the Most High. The Lord God will give him the throne of his father David, and he will reign over Jacob's descendants forever; his kingdom will never end."

"How will this be?" I asked the angel. "I am a virgin."

This great being of light answered, "The Holy Spirit will come on you, and the power of the Most High will overshadow you. So the holy one to be born will be called the Son of God. Even Elizabeth your relative is going to have a child in her old age, and she who was said to be unable to conceive is in her sixth month. For no word from God will ever fail."

Words came to my mind, like some refrain I had heard long ago. "I am the Lord's servant," I answered. "May your word to me be fulfilled." Then the angel left in a fiery flash, as if from a fierce and mighty storm.

I struggled for breath. I could not go back to the spindle, and yet I could not rest. I was stirred to tears—wonderment and fear filled my heart. I, Mary, would give birth to a son! But my betrothed and his family? What would they do? What would they say? And my own family—could they fathom such a marvel, or would they be pierced with sorrow?

I shuddered to think of what the law allowed, what might happen to me. And yet . . . the angel had said I had found favor with God. Surely his word could be trusted. Surely his word would not fail. I am the servant of the Lord, and with him I will let my faith rest. I will place my life in his care.

I pondered all the angel had foretold. I had no need to strain for his words, for they were burned forever on my heart. Though I did not know it then, those words would always reside there and be a comfort to me, through the coming months, through the life and death of my firstborn, and all the years to come.

But then all I knew was my village, my quiet home, my family. My thoughts turned to dear Elizabeth, in her sixth month. *How merciful, Lord!*

I gazed at my rough hands, at the simple grey wool of my tunic. I was just a poor girl. No more than a peasant from Nazareth. And yet somehow I knew the angel's words would come to pass.

> *I was stirred to tears—wonderment and fear filled my heart. I, Mary, would give birth to a son!*

I placed my hands over my womb. I would be the mother to the noblest of all earthly sons. Jesus . . . God saves. My child. My son would be the long-awaited Messiah!

My heart burst with joy and song:

> My soul glorifies the Lord
> and my spirit rejoices in God my Savior,
> for he has been mindful
> of the humble state of his servant.
> From now on all generations will call me blessed,
> for the Mighty One has done great things for me—
> holy is his name!

A peace-filled awe covered my spirit as I raised my hands to the Lord, praising him for this gift—this unfathomable miracle for all mankind.

THE STORY FROM GOD'S WORD

LUKE 1:26-38

In the sixth month of Elizabeth's pregnancy, God sent the angel Gabriel to Nazareth, a town in Galilee, to a virgin pledged to be married to a man named Joseph, a descendant of David. The virgin's name was Mary. The angel went to her and said, "Greetings, you who are highly favored! The Lord is with you."

Mary was greatly troubled at his words and wondered what kind of greeting this might be. But the angel said to her, "Do not be afraid, Mary; you have found favor with God. You will conceive and give birth to a son, and you are to call him Jesus. He will be great and will be called the Son of the Most High. The Lord God will give him the throne of his father David, and he will reign over Jacob's descendants forever; his kingdom will never end."

"How will this be," Mary asked the angel, "since I am a virgin?"

The angel answered, "The Holy Spirit will come on you, and the power of the Most High will overshadow you. So the holy one to be born will be called the Son of God. Even Elizabeth your relative is going to have a child in her old age, and she who was said to be unable to conceive is in her sixth month. For no word from God will ever fail."

"I am the Lord's servant," Mary answered. "May your word to me be fulfilled." Then the angel left her.

> *Can you imagine being singled out in such a way by the Creator of the universe?*

THE STORY—FROM THEN TO NOW

According to what is understood from Scripture and what scholars know about the culture of the time, Mary was a young girl—perhaps twelve or thirteen—when God sent Gabriel to her. It would have been understandable for her to be frightened, as well as joyous and mystified, at the angel's announcement that day. Mary's family would not have expected such attention. They were peasant folk, and except for the lineage of King David, they had no worldly prestige. From those looking on, Mary's lowly position must have made her seem like an unlikely choice for such a sacred and glorious task—to assist in the earthly entrance of the King of kings and Lord of lords!

But Mary had been chosen by the Almighty. Can you imagine being singled out in such a way by the Creator of the universe? Hard to fathom such an honor. Mary must have gone through a wide range of emotions as she contemplated her unique predicament, and as she later felt the holy child grow within her womb. Mary did, however, prove herself worthy of this heavy charge.

Even though our work may not seem as exalted as Mary's, God gives us each important responsibilities. In fact, some of his requests may look immense and impossible from our earthly point of view. For me personally, one seemingly hopeless task comes to mind. At an early age God gave me the desire to write, but for years I kept refusing to follow through with the dream— a dream I knew he'd placed in my heart. Unfortunately, I had come to mistakenly believe that God had given me a blueprint for my life, but had forgotten to give me the tools and materials I needed to build the dream into a reality. Now I know that my poor confidence was really just a disguise for my lack of trust in God.

When I finally agreed to become a writer, I would like to say that my life suddenly cruised along with relatively few bumps, but just like Mary and anyone else on a divine errand, victory did not come easily. I had a rough road much of the time. I still know, however, that writing is what God wanted me to do, what he's gifted me to do, and so I feel grateful and honored to be on this journey with him.

Throughout the Bible God used ordinary people to accomplish extraordinary things. I promise you that whatever he's commissioned you to do, he'll give you the tools and the stamina and the heart to accomplish it. With God's help Mary accepted her calling and took the seemingly impassable road, and it led to the birth of a King who changed the course of the entire world. We too need that simple trust, that humble obedience to follow his lead even when the rough road ahead looks like it's been hit with a meteor shower.

So . . . what's God calling *you* to do?

❧ THE STORY ❧
QUESTIONS TO THINK ABOUT

1. When the angel first appeared to Mary, what do you think her first thoughts might have been? What would you have thought if an angel had appeared to you when you were a teenager?

2. If the angel's glorious news had been for you, what would your reaction have been? Would you have said you were the Lord's servant? Why or why not?

3. What do you think Mary's family said to her when they found out about her pregnancy? What do we know about Joseph's initial reaction to the news of Mary's condition? How do you think this news affected her relationships with other people?

4. What clues do we have in Scripture about the way Mary felt about this child?

5. We don't all see angels, and none of us will give birth to the Messiah, but what do you find in Mary's story that relates to your life? What about her story, her words, or her emotions is most meaningful to you?

6. Has God given you a special task? Have you said yes to him and trusted God, as Mary did? If you have, how has that affected your life? If you haven't, what has held you back?

❧ FOUR ❧

Peter

When he saw the wind, he was afraid and,
beginning to sink, cried out, "Lord, save me!"

MATTHEW 14:30

here was no escape. The howling winds tormented us as if they were made by a great winged devil, fixed on capsizing our boat. We lowered the sail, and I battled against the oars until my arms gave in to the fire searing its way through my flesh.

I looked out over the brooding deep, praying for a waning of the gale, but none came. The waves propelled us upward and then swept us down into the sea's heaving bowels. The oak hull, no matter how strong, would never hold. We would surely perish in the sea!

When I thought my horror could not swell any greater, I caught sight of an image floating upon the surface of the water, just visible in the lingering starlight and the pale glow before dawn. I quaked within, but did not mention the apparition to the others.

Fear rose in my belly, filling my mouth with a taste like bitter herbs. Could this vision come from my weariness, or a frailty in spirit? I prayed, willing the ghost to vanish, but it remained, calmly moving across the very waves we battled!

My brothers ceased rowing and surveyed the water. They

screamed in terror. "It's a ghost," several of them said. At the sound of these words, the boat came to life with chaos and shouts.

And then a voice rolled over the waves like thunder: "Take courage! It is I. Don't be afraid."

My Lord? How can this be? Walking on the waves? Even before I grasped the marvel of what I witnessed, I called out to him. "Lord, if it's you, tell me to come to you on the water."

A moment later he replied, "Come."

Yes, Lord. I will. In a feverish flash of conviction and love for my Lord, I climbed over the side of the boat. Just before my hands let go, my courage ebbed, and my limbs weakened with terror. For an instant I strained to climb back into the boat. But lest my brothers laugh at my cowardice, I dropped myself down into the undulating waves. Even though the waters surged and splashed around me, I was not pulled under. Praise be to God— my feet felt as steady as if rooted in the hills of Galilee!

But as I moved farther away from the boat, winds lashed at me, beating my tunic and cloak against my flesh. For a moment, I turned away from my Master and stared into the churning sea. My heart lurched at the sight of the dark mystery, the great unknown. *What a fool I was!*

> *And then a voice rolled over the waves like thunder: "Take courage! It is I. Don't be afraid."*

My fears gathered like scavengers over the smell of death. Right away I began to sink, and the waves opened like the jaws of Hades. I choked on a gulp of water and fought my way to the surface. A cluster of stars shone with an alluring brightness, tempting me to call out to the heavenly bodies for my salvation. But I called out to my Master instead. "Lord, save me!"

Jesus was suddenly by my side. He reached out his hand and from the waters lifted me. The look in his eyes was one of benevolent rebuke. "You of little faith," he said to me, "why did you doubt?"

Forgive me, Lord. My spirit tore into pieces at the knowledge of what I had done. Yet as he helped me into the boat, the winds calmed over the dark sea, and my soul was stilled by his forgiveness. As my brothers attended to us, I struggled with a new and bewildering conviction—a knowing deep in my spirit that the demon of doubt was not yet finished with me . . .

But in that moment, watching my Lord smile and greet my brothers, my heart swelled with praise. We all bowed in worship, saying to him, "Truly, you are the Son of God!"

THE STORY FROM GOD'S WORD
MATTHEW 14:22-33

Immediately Jesus made the disciples get into the boat and go on ahead of him to the other side, while he dismissed the crowd. After he had dismissed them, he went up on a mountainside by himself to pray. Later that night, he was there alone, and the boat was already a considerable distance from land, buffeted by the waves because the wind was against it.

Shortly before dawn Jesus went out to them, walking on the lake. When the disciples saw him walking on the lake, they were terrified. "It's a ghost," they said, and cried out in fear.

But Jesus immediately said to them: "Take courage! It is I. Don't be afraid."

"Lord, if it's you," Peter replied, "tell me to come to you on the water."

"Come," he said.

Then Peter got down out of the boat, walked on the water and came toward Jesus. But when he saw the wind, he was afraid and, beginning to sink, cried out, "Lord, save me!"

Immediately Jesus reached out his hand and caught him. "You of little faith," he said, "why did you doubt?"

And when they climbed into the boat, the wind died down. Then those who were in the boat worshiped him, saying, "Truly you are the Son of God."

THE STORY—FROM THEN TO NOW

In Peter's story I am always gripped by his wild nature. His swashbuckling spirit. His bold affection for his Master. Peter is the king of impetuosity!

I wonder what the other disciples thought of his sudden leap into the perilous waves. Did they know him well enough to say, "There goes Peter . . . he's at it again"? Or were they always surprised by his full-throttle approach to life?

I'm sure we all have our moments of rash decisions and impulsive words. I am guilty of both. This weakness has gotten me into all sorts of squirmy predicaments over the years. For instance, my desire to be gracious is sometimes overridden by my need to make an all-important point. But sometimes the point I'm making may have a sharp end on it, pricking the heart of the person I'm intending to grace with my vital opinion! So, invariably, God finds a gentle way to humble me into an apology.

> *I'm sure we all have our moments of rash decisions and impulsive words. I am guilty of both.*

I see that gentle way in Peter's story as well. I'm moved by how the Lord dealt with Peter's temperament. He simply said, "Come." Jesus could have said, "I know you're going to start doubting, Peter, and then you're going to sink like the rock you're named after." But Jesus didn't say that. He just said, "Come."

God always wants our faith to stand strong, and yet free will is a part of his sovereign plan. That does not mean when sin comes calling that we should put a welcome sign over our heart's door. But when we do fall, he can redeem our failures for his purpose and glory. This means reproof and hopefully growth. His Word says those he loves, he rebukes. Since that's the case, I must be truly loved!

Later in Peter's story, he did wrestle with the demons of doubt and fear again. But Jesus also said to him, "On this rock I will build my church." How utterly noble and triumphant-sounding is that?

In the end, with God's helping hand, Peter rose above his weaknesses. That overcoming power is available to us too. Even though having free will means we may indeed falter and sink, that doesn't have to be the end of our stories. The Almighty gives Christians the Holy Spirit so that when we hear Jesus say, "Come," we'll be able to climb out of the boat, stay focused on the Master, and walk on water.

⚘ THE STORY ⚘
QUESTIONS TO THINK ABOUT

1. Peter was the only disciple to get out of the boat and walk toward Jesus. What do you think made him want to walk on the water like Jesus?

2. Peter took his eyes off Jesus and became so full of fear that he began to sink into the sea. Think of an instance in your life when you felt like Peter. What was the "wind" you saw that took away your courage?

3. What does it say to you about Peter that he challenged the "ghost" to prove himself to be Jesus? What impression do you get about the other men in the boat?

4. Throughout the Gospels and elsewhere in the New Testament, Peter appeared to be rather impulsive in nature. How was that a strength for him? How was it a weakness?

5. Jesus said of Peter, "On this rock I will build my church" (the Greek word for Peter means "rock"; Matthew 16:18). If that sentence had been at the end of this story about walking on water, we might think Jesus was being sarcastic. What does it tell you about Jesus that he picked such an unsteady person to be his "rock"? Do you think strength can come from doubt? Why or why not?

6. Jesus said, "Take courage!" What does this story teach you about courage?

FIVE

Leah

*But she said to her, "Wasn't it enough that
you took away my husband?"*
GENESIS 30:15

M y eyes beheld Reuben's gift to me—the treasured
mandrake plants.

The veined leaves unfolded like ancient hands, the
roots stretched out before me like the limbs of a woman, and the
ripened fruit smelled pleasant and spicy. The mandrakes were
precious to me, and yet in the sanctuary of my heart I knew they
were even more pernicious.

I looked toward my son as he walked back through the sway-
ing fields of golden wheat. Just as Reuben returned to his sickle,
I saw my sister, Rachel—Jacob's jewel—coming toward me. Her
purposeful stride warned me that she had seen Reuben's gift,
and she wanted it. I clutched the plants close to my breast as she
approached.

Rachel, as devious in spirit as she was beautiful to be-
hold, inquired of me, "Leah, please give me some of Reuben's
mandrakes."

I backed away. I tried to hold my tongue, but my mouth
filled with bitterness. "Wasn't it enough that you took away my
husband? Will you take my son's mandrakes too?"

Rachel coveted my plants, for the numinous roots and fruit.

For even though the mandrake could be as deadly as a viper's sting, it could also claim powerful and mystical properties that were said to cure a barren womb. And Rachel—Jacob's precious pearl—had no sons. She was as fruitful as a dead fig tree, and she would do anything to possess the mandrakes.

"Very well," Rachel stepped toward me. Her eyes narrowed like a lazy camel. "Jacob can lie down with you tonight in return for the mandrakes."

Rachel was better at scheming and moving her tongue than she was at moving the millstone. Like the wheat around us, my sister would benefit mightily from a good threshing! But I agreed to Rachel's plot and handed her half of my beloved mandrakes.

She left me there in the field, and I stared after her, despairing over the jealousy that tormented us. But even more, I grieved over the bitter truth that blistered my heart; I was the one left unloved. Why was I born without beauty—born without those bewitching onyx eyes—to be forsaken, without honor, without love?

My desire for some magic remedy for my heartache pierced me, and I was ashamed. Hadn't God heard my solemn cries? Hadn't he understood my misery and seen fit to grant me four healthy sons? And yet I had turned from him once again.

As I had done a thousand times before, I conjured up my wedding day and the marriage bed—how I'd hidden behind my veil, secreted myself from the light. My father's command for me was to say nothing to Jacob until our first morning as man and wife. Jacob had not wanted me then, as he did not want me now.

My father deceived my husband, and so I became a woeful weight on Jacob's spirit—displeasing in his sight, a servant not to be treasured as gold or silver but to be merely endured. I felt the burden of my name, which means "weary." And weary I was of my lot.

So, I have revered the mandrakes too, even though God has graced me with sons. Perhaps my Lord would see my use of the plant as a betrayal. As a mockery of his generosity. Have I failed to trust him in this season of a quiet womb?

A lonely disgrace ran through my soul as a crimson stain runs through fine linen. I knew God would desire me to feel pity for Rachel, forgiving her for the years of envy and pride. Since in the end, I would surely gain Jacob's love. I crushed a mandrake berry between my fingers and watched the juice fall to the dust. In the end, I would be remembered for the great tribes that would rise from the fruit of my body. From the favor and everlasting mercy of the Almighty.

> *She left me there in the field, and I stared after her, despairing over the jealousy that tormented us.*

THE STORY FROM GOD'S WORD
GENESIS 30:14-17

During wheat harvest, Reuben went out into the fields and found some mandrake plants, which he brought to his mother Leah. Rachel said to Leah, "Please give me some of your son's mandrakes."

But she said to her, "Wasn't it enough that you took away my husband? Will you take my son's mandrakes too?"

"Very well," Rachel said, "he can sleep with you tonight in return for your son's mandrakes."

So when Jacob came in from the fields that evening, Leah went out to meet him. "You must sleep with me," she said. "I have hired you with my son's mandrakes." So he slept with her that night.

God listened to Leah, and she became pregnant and bore Jacob a fifth son.

THE STORY—FROM THEN TO NOW

The story of Leah and Rachel deals with a multitude of sins—reshaping God, polygamy, and jealousy. Sounds a little like a scene from *Desperate Housewives*!

I think the story of Leah shows us vividly why polygamy doesn't work, and why that lifestyle was never God's intention for men and women. But sexual sins are only part of the problematic issues played out in this biblical soap opera. The fact that Leah and Rachel appeared to be dabbling in a rather mystical and superstitious method of conceiving, instead of totally relying on God's power, tells us something about their levels of faith.

> *Resentment is a universally acknowledged sentiment, and it doesn't appear just when two women are fighting for the love of a man.*

But for now, let's talk about the blaze of jealousy that burned its way through the sisterhood of Leah and Rachel. In this passage it becomes obvious what the two women are feeling—they don't want to share their husband. They both want to be his one and only. They both want to be the twinkle in Jacob's eye. They both want to claim the full honor of being the wife of Jacob, son of Isaac, son of Abraham. But polygamy makes that impossible, so the baby battle begins. Their war goes to the extreme, including using each other's servants as breeding machines. Imagine!

But jealousy is like the china that we bring out for all sorts of special occasions. Resentment is a universally acknowledged sentiment, and it doesn't appear just when two women are fighting for the love of a man. I've also had an up-close and personal encounter with this heated emotion, and I've gotten burned and charred more times than I'm willing to say.

For instance, in the writing profession, as in others, you can always find someone who is more successful than you are. More book deals, bigger sales. Better advance money. More prestigious awards. You name it. No matter how hard you work or how smart you are, there will always be plenty of folks who are able to one-up you at a gathering of writers. There's always that person who's jetting out to L. A. to see the première of her latest novel, while whining about her paltry, six-figure advance. I'm being a little over-the-top here, but you get my drift. I do pray I've moved beyond the petty spiritual entanglements of this kind of envy. But from time to time, I still have to seek God's forgiveness in this area of my life.

The one thing I love most about Rachel and Leah's story is that, no matter how the characters sullied their lives, God still cherished them and came to their rescue when they cried out to him. Leah and Rachel both wanted children in the worst way, and God fulfilled their hearts' desires. Leah wanted her husband to love her, and even though the story doesn't give us that information, I would like to believe that God, in his infinite mercy, granted her love.

For us today, I find it most comforting to know that, no matter how far we wander off God's story line, his fellowship is just a prayer away.

❧ THE STORY ☙
QUESTIONS TO THINK ABOUT

1. Most modern women cannot relate to polygamy, but we can all understand the feelings of envy and jealousy. When have you felt these emotions?

2. What, if anything, has ever led your feelings to become something worse, such as hatred, or even hateful actions?

3. What, if anything, has helped you to deal with these surges of emotion in a healthy way, or has helped you avoid them altogether?

4. The sin of polygamy created impossible situations for women, back then and today. People are faced with all kinds of difficult situations that are often not of their own making. How can we deal with the consequences of someone else's sin when it has an impact on us personally?

5. Leah was unloved by her husband, and she cried out to the Lord to have children. God heard her plea and honored her request. Have you ever felt like Leah? When and how have you felt that God has come to your rescue?

6. It seemed as though Rachel and Leah and Jacob made a mess of their lives, and yet God worked powerfully in the midst of their transgressions. Do you think God still works the same way today? Give an example of a time when you failed God, but he remained faithful, showing you his tender love in spite of your sin.

SIX

The Man at Bethesda

He asked him, "Do you want to get well?"
JOHN 5:6

I rested on my mat, dreaming of Eden. A garden sanctuary, so we are told. A place full of beauty, full of endless days, and full of God. Where life was sweeter than wild honey, where the sky never clouded with misery, and limbs never hardened to stone.

But when I opened my eyes, I did not reside in Eden. I was resting by the healing pool of Bethesda, where I came each day with hope in my spirit; and where day after day I became more ragged with despair.

The blind and the infirm surrounded me, and yet I was alone. People crowded me and crushed me. They ignored me. My name is Enosh, but I am nameless. I am like the buried dead, unclean to many, unseen by all.

I stared into the colonnades as I had countless times, and then I gazed up into the firmament above. *My Lord, what have I done?* I wondered. Had I committed some black and unpardonable sin that I would find myself in such sorrow, such brokenness? Was there a curse placed on me as a child? I had cried a thousand prayers, tears enough to fill heaven, and yet they'd fallen back down as dry as bones in the desert. I was invisible even to God. After years of breathing in the stench of filth and rotting flesh, how could I endure this house of shame any longer? This synagogue of Satan—my own frail body.

At that moment someone stepped very near me. I looked up at what had shadowed the sun and found the dark eyes of a man who not only looked at me but truly saw me. They were eyes flashing with fire and lit with love. It was as if I were staring into all the starry host.

The stranger said to me, "Do you want to get well?"

"Sir," I replied, "I have no one to help me into the pool when the water is stirred. While I am trying to get in, someone else goes down ahead of me."

Then this stranger commanded, "Get up! Pick up your mat and walk."

What could I do but obey? I reached down to my limbs and felt the blood of life spilling through my veins. The marvel of sensation—of pain. Blessed pain! Without the hands of others lifting me, I pulled up my legs. My body surged with awakening. I hoisted myself up, picked up my mat, and took a step like a tottering calf. I slapped my face to make certain I wasn't dreaming again.

But it was not a dream. I began leaping and rejoicing. "Praise to God for his mercy. I am healed!" I had no need for the troubling waters. No need for the pool by the Sheep Gate. I needed no one to carry me like a child. I was whole!

The crowd circled around me, watching my every step. Some of them cheered, "Isn't that the man who could not walk?" But some of them scowled and grumbled in envy. A few of the Jewish leaders came toward me, lathering with sanctimonious inquiries, their noses held so high they could catch a swarm of gnats. But I brushed by their pious pomp in desperate search for the man who had healed me—the man who *saw* me. I turned this way and that, still shouting praises, but the stranger had slipped through the crowd. Perhaps he was weary of the mob, of the heat. Who was he? I wanted to thank him.

I placed my hands over my heart and stared back into the swirling vault of heaven. This moment—the day God saw me—would remain in my mind as a moment full of beauty, full of endlessness, and full of God.

This time as I thought of Eden, I stood.

THE STORY FROM GOD'S WORD
JOHN 5:1-9

Some time later, Jesus went up to Jerusalem for one of the Jewish festivals. Now there is in Jerusalem near the Sheep Gate a pool, which in Aramaic is called Bethesda and which is surrounded by five covered colonnades. Here a great number of disabled people used to lie—the blind, the lame, the paralyzed. One who was there had been an invalid for thirty-eight years. When Jesus saw him lying there and learned that he had been in this condition for a long time, he asked him, "Do you want to get well?"

"Sir," the invalid replied, "I have no one to help me into the pool when the water is stirred. While I am trying to get in, someone else goes down ahead of me."

Then Jesus said to him, "Get up! Pick up your mat and walk." At once the man was cured; he picked up his mat and walked.

THE STORY—FROM THEN TO NOW

It's hard not to love this story in the Bible about the man at the healing pool. This story gets to us because we love to see the underdog prevail, to witness joy carved out of despair. And this poor crippled man had despaired for thirty-eight years, waiting for his miracle. Waiting for someone to see him.

There seems to be quite a paradox surrounding miracles—we are to expect them, but they are not always guaranteed. I admit, I get weary at times when I see no improvement in the people whom I've prayed for over and over. It's easy to secretly give up. It's less complicated and less painful to abandon hope than to constantly be perched on the edge of life, holding one's breath, waiting for all to be made right. It may be easier to give up, but it's not the way of faith.

The Enemy would like nothing better than for us to walk away from hope. To drop our expectations so low that we are reduced to picking at the petty crumbs of life, while we miss a whole banquet of miracles before us. Ever since the Garden of Eden, people have been overlooking what is eternal for what is temporal. We've traded the immortal for the mundane. When we are busy staring at the dirt, we don't have time to look up from the mire to witness the divine. We can no longer believe in miracles. And perhaps we cannot even recognize them when they finally arrive, even though there are daily supernatural wonders all around us.

One helpful discipline might be to keep a journal of miracles. Some time ago I kept track of our family's answers to prayers for a year. I wrote them down in one of those pretty little notebooks that people give you (that you have no idea what to do with). Anyway, at the end of the year I was amazed at how many miracles had accumulated in that little book. Some were small, some big. But all were miracles.

Ever since the Garden of Eden, people have been overlooking what is eternal for what is temporal.

I do need to add one caveat; these miracles rarely came exactly when I wanted them, and they weren't delivered in the way I imagined. Truly his ways are not our ways, and we don't understand the timing of events. Some miracles happen immediately, some are stayed, and others are resolved in the arms of Jesus.

Unfortunately, this isn't the Garden of Eden—it's now a sinful and fallen world. But God's mercy endures forever. He cared enough to come to earth and make the ultimate sacrifice for us. Jesus' resurrection after his death on the cross is still the biggest and best miracle of all time, and it's the ultimate reminder to never give up hope—to know that God is still active in every part of our lives. That the God of the universe still sees us, even when nothing makes sense, and even when all seems lost.

What miracle are you waiting for?

✄ THE STORY ✄
QUESTIONS TO THINK ABOUT

1. In this story, when Jesus asked the man at the pool at Bethesda if he wanted to get well, the man explained why he wasn't being healed. Jesus didn't discuss the waters at Bethesda—whether or not they had healing powers—but just told the man to get up. Why do you think that Jesus handled the healing in this way, bypassing the man's explanation?

2. Later in the story of the man at the pool, he is chastised by the Jewish leaders for doing the work of carrying something (his mat) on the Sabbath. They don't even seem to acknowledge the healing that has occurred—they are just concerned about a rule violation. What do you think the Gospel writer is trying to show us about Jesus through this story? What is he saying about the Jewish leaders?

3. The man at the pool had come back over and over, hoping to be healed in the waters. His discouragement must have been acute by the time Jesus found him. Have you ever reached the point of giving up hope? What happened?

4. Why do you think God heals some people and others are still suffering? Some say the latter is from a lack of faith, but is that thinking biblically sound? Explain your answer.

5. Miracles do happen in our lives. Some are seen and some are unseen. Have you ever experienced a miracle that you didn't know about until years later? What happened?

6. The Enemy, Satan, wants us to give up hope. What are some ways to keep hope alive while we're waiting on God's answer to our prayers?

SEVEN

Pilate's Wife

*While Pilate was sitting on the judge's seat,
his wife sent him this message: "Don't have
anything to do with that innocent man."*
MATTHEW 27:19

I awakened, tasting my own blood. While in deep slumber, I had bitten my tongue. A dream most gruesome had ravaged my sleep, and a feverish dampness shrouded my body. I untangled myself from my coverings, moved to the side of my bed, and spit into a bowl. I sipped some wine from a goblet and then hastily drank the rest of it down.

This dream was not like any other, but born of supernatural means and full of dark omens. It was as if my sleeping and my waking were held together with the scarlet ribbon of death!

I gazed around my bedchamber. Except for the remnants of terror in my mind, all was quiet. In my dream I had glimpsed through a forbidden curtain. My spirit wanted to flee, but where could it go? I clung to my bedpost, trembling.

In my mind a whirling wind had come and swept my husband away. When I saw him again, he stood on the rim of a great precipice. We were forever separated by a bottomless abyss, and yet I could see him well. His eyes gaped at me, the sockets hollow and coiling with a gangrenous vapor. His hands appeared withered and encrusted with dried blood. It was the blood of an innocent man, a man my husband in his duties as prefect would soon sentence to death. The man would die by crucifixion—a violent and agonizing end. Then in the dream, my husband lunged off the edge of the cliff. A look of terror crossed his features as he fell into the abyss.

> *If I do not speak of this, then the guilt will be on my head.*

I wiped the dampness from my face, longing to wipe away the dreadful images. A dazzling light poured through my window. And then a darkness, filled with the foul fragrance of the underworld, slithered in until it blotted out the dawn light. What manner of presence had entered my chambers? Whispers came to me in a hot, sulfurous-laden breath, "Jesus must not die." I clutched at my ears, desperate to silence the hissing sounds. Perhaps I no longer had my mind. Was I as mad as the women who carried on in the streets—the women who were plagued by spirits? Or had this visitation been an omen from the gods?

If I do not speak of this, then the guilt will be on my head. I called to my maidservant. I could get a message to my husband. Tell him of my dream. Change the course of events.

But my mind felt riddled with confusion over the condemned prophet, Jesus. Why did the Jews hail him as Lord and then demand to have him crucified? Why such a violent uprising over such a harmless man? What danger was he to Rome? Simply because of his claim to be the Messiah of the Jews? He was not truly a king or judge or god. I trembled again.

But what if this man were more?

A pearl of blood had dropped from my lips, soiling my linen robe. I tore the garment off, and yet I felt the scarlet stain upon my skin. No amount of pure water would make me clean. No sacrifice to the gods could save me from this terror.

Where is that lazy servant of mine! But as I called out to her again, thunder rolled through my bedchamber and shook me to my bones. The wind murmured through the open window, but this time I sensed another truth. I have gone to the shrines, and I have sacrificed and appeased and sworn by the gods all my days—deities that cannot speak, idols that cannot hear. Gods that are not gods at all, but stone. *Who will I turn to?*

My maidservant rushed into my chamber. Distraught in my uncertainty and fear, I sent her away with my message.

The Story from God's Word
Matthew 27:15-20

Now it was the governor's custom at the festival to release a prisoner chosen by the crowd. At that time they had a well-known prisoner whose name was Jesus Barabbas. So when the crowd had gathered, Pilate asked them, "Which one do you want me to release to you: Jesus Barabbas, or Jesus who is called Messiah?" For he knew it was out of self-interest that they had handed Jesus over to him.

While Pilate was sitting on the judge's seat, his wife sent him this message: "Don't have anything to do with that innocent man, for I have suffered a great deal today in a dream because of him."

But the chief priests and the elders persuaded the crowd to ask for Barabbas and to have Jesus executed.

The Story—from Then to Now

We've all had bad dreams, but the nightmare Pilate's wife experienced may have come from supernatural influences—that is, Satan, in his dark attempt to keep Jesus from his death and resurrection. The irony in this story is that Pilate's wife thought she needed to rescue Jesus, but the reason for his coming was to save humanity.

Jesus' return from the grave changed everything. It was proof of his rule over death's fearful grip. Evidence of his sovereignty over all the earth. His final say in what mattered most—forgiveness and the opportunity to have the crown of life, that is, to join the Lord in heaven for all time. This kind of grace and eternal fellowship with God is not what the Enemy wants for our souls.

This battle for our souls is centered on one person and one victory—Jesus and what happened on Easter morning. Through his willing sacrifice and resurrection, we have been offered redemption, the gift that Satan wanted to deny us. Along with that salvation comes the enjoyment of God's friendship and love and his beautiful creation for all eternity. If you've not accepted these generous presents, I pray that you will.

✢ THE STORY ✢
QUESTIONS TO THINK ABOUT

1. Pilate's wife had a dream about Jesus—one that revealed his innocence. Throughout the Bible we see clearly the existence of spiritual warfare. Do you think this dream about Jesus' innocence came from Satan or from God? Explain your answer.

2. Have you ever had a sense of foreboding about a situation? How do you think you can discern whether a dream or a feeling is something you should pay attention to or ignore?

3. How do you think Pilate's wife felt when she realized her husband had ignored her warning?

4. Pilate and his wife had a unique encounter with Jesus. How do you think this encounter with Christ might have impacted their lives after the resurrection?

5. Pilate acted against his own judgment and against the warning of his wife when he released Barabbas. Though he seemed to be in a position of power, he caved to the shouts of the crowd and the politics of the Jewish leaders. Have you ever chosen a way contrary to your judgment because of outside pressure? What kinds of pressures have the greatest influence on you?

6. Pilate's wife has a very small role in the drama of Jesus' trial, but still she is there. What purpose do you think her dream serves in this story?

7. What part of this story is the most compelling to you, and why?

EIGHT

Lazarus

He was deeply moved in spirit and troubled.
JOHN 11:33

My heart vaulted as if struck by lightning. Its beat thundered within me. Light blazed before my eyes, and fire coursed through the cold ruins of my flesh, igniting my innermost being. I awakened, gasping and fighting for air. Then a great wheezing sigh left my lungs. I was in the earth, quaking. I was . . . alive.

A putrid odor overpowered me. *Am I among the living or the dead? Has a dream engulfed my soul?* But it was no pagan trance or vision from a deep slumber that afflicted me.

Someone had shouted my name—someone had commanded me into existence.

Suspended between the high places of the living and the valley of the dead, I had soared with the angels on borrowed wings. I had counted the stars. And from a distance, with green pastures stretched between us, I had seen Abraham.

Memories came forth like a spring burbling up through the rocks. There had been wailing sounds of mourning all around me. There was darkness, and then there was light. Such light that no man, except for Moses, had ever beheld. I had known the resplendence of an ageless dwelling—of time without end. I had crossed over the everlasting barrier.

My body shifted. A voice, a power, had charged me to come forth! I lifted my hand, but it felt heavy as if it had been tied to a millstone. I lifted my head from its resting place. Pain stung my skull, like a thousand biting hornets. I blinked open my eyes, but could see little through the cloth covering my face. Where was I? A cave, no doubt—a place to bury the dead. Then without my own force of will, a sudden and profound strength overtook me. I rose from the bier and swayed and lurched toward the faint light—the mouth of the open tomb.

I would see my family again, my sisters, Mary and Martha. The grand feast of life would be laid before me, and I would savor it anew. I would witness the birds taking flight and the beasts in the field. The songs of the desert would be mine. The rise and fall of the seasons, seedtime and harvest, winter and summer, would once again rule the rhythm of my years.

When I stumbled out of the tomb and into the daylight, screams of terror and shouts of joy greeted me. A voice I recognized said, "Take off the grave clothes and let him go."

Hands tore at the wrappings, rending the linen strips from my body. Once my face was freed from the cloth, I saw my beloved friend—the man to whom I owed my life—Jesus.

The crowd waited, silent and still, for me to speak. With my mouth parched as dust, I said, "Praise you . . . Lord, my God." And then I raised my voice to a shout, "I am among the living. As King David said, 'My heart is glad and my tongue rejoices; my body also will rest secure, because you will not abandon me to the realm of the dead!'"

The Story from God's Word

John 11:33-44

When Jesus saw her weeping, and the Jews who had come along with her also weeping, he was deeply moved in spirit and troubled. "Where have you laid him?" he asked.

"Come and see, Lord," they replied.

Jesus wept.

Then the Jews said, "See how he loved him!"

But some of them said, "Could not he who opened the eyes of the blind man have kept this man from dying?"

Jesus, once more deeply moved, came to the tomb. It was a cave with a stone laid across the entrance. "Take away the stone," he said.

"But, Lord," said Martha, the sister of the dead man, "by this time there is a bad odor, for he has been there four days."

Then Jesus said, "Did I not tell you that if you believe, you will see the glory of God?"

So they took away the stone. Then Jesus looked up and said, "Father, I thank you that you have heard me. I knew that you always hear me, but I said this for the benefit of the people standing here, that they may believe that you sent me."

When he had said this, Jesus called in a loud voice, "Lazarus, come out!" The dead man came out, his hands and feet wrapped with strips of linen, and a cloth around his face.

Jesus said to them, "Take off the grave clothes and let him go."

> He is a God of justice and judgment, but he's also a God of great empathy.

THE STORY—FROM THEN TO NOW

Have you ever gone through a dark season in your life? I call it the black flood—when everything in your life is stirring in a cauldron of misery. Perhaps you've known the loss of a beloved friendship, or a job, or your health. Or maybe a family member seems intent on going the way of destruction. The list could go on for pages. But I think the one thing we crave the most in these impossible times—that is, besides an immediate end to our problems—is compassion.

Where can we find it? Some people seem to have the spiritual gift of compassion in our time of need. Others only offer us deadpan stares. And sometimes those who are gifted with compassion seem to be holding back on us. When even the best friend fails us, I hope we can remember the brief but powerful Scripture earlier in this story: "Jesus wept." This one tiny sentence gives us a beautiful glimpse at another facet of our Lord's character. He is a God of justice and judgment, but he's also a God of great empathy.

Martha and Mary were obviously devastated over their brother's death, and when Jesus saw their anguish, he broke down and cried. Think of it—the Creator of the world shed tears for one of his creation. He knows well that this life is full of many trials. He lived through our earthly trials, more than you or I will ever experience in our lifetimes, but he also overcame the world. He went through that horrendous gauntlet of suffering just for you, and just for me. So, when you pass through the black flood of trials, know that God is full of compassion. He weeps for us. And beyond that emotional compassion, he promises never to leave us or forsake us. Draw from that comforting knowledge whenever you have need.

⅍ THE STORY ⅍
QUESTIONS TO THINK ABOUT

1. People seek signs and wonders. Lazarus rising from the dead was one of the most dramatic episodes in the Bible. Why do you think some of the people who witnessed that extraordinary marvel were still skeptical about Jesus' identity? (Read John 11:45-48.)

2. "Jesus wept" (John 11:35) is the shortest verse in the Bible, but it's also one of the most revealing. Why do you think Jesus would cry over his friend's death when he knew he would bring him back to life?

3. How does it make you feel to know Jesus wept over the death of his friend? How does that impact what you think about the experience of grief?

4. When Jesus asked them to take away the stone from Lazarus's grave, Martha said to the Lord about the body of her brother, "by this time there is a bad odor, for he has been there four days." Martha knew Jesus was Lord, but she still doubted his plan. Try to put yourself in Martha's shoes. What do you think you would have done or said?

5. Why do you think it is so difficult for us to trust Jesus with our earthly lives, even when we firmly believe he is our Savior?

6. What is your favorite part of Lazarus's story, and why?

NINE

Hagar

*Then she went off and sat down about
a bowshot away, for she thought,
"I cannot watch the boy die."*

GENESIS 21:16

Alone and abandoned, we would surely die in the desert. I offered my son, Ishmael, the skin of water, and he drank the last few drops. He fell against me, limp and weary, his body drained of life. His young and princely face had turned red from the sun, and his lips were parched white from thirst. As I held him to me, he tucked his face into the curve of my neck, as he had done when he was a baby. I wept silent tears, not wanting him to see my sorrow, not wanting him to know that we would breathe our last in this wilderness.

Ishmael looked up at me for comfort then. I had none to give him. His spirit still trusted, but mine was as worthless as a clay pot smashed against the rocks.

I gazed around, hoping for some small relief from our torment. In the distance on the side of a dusty hill a goat bleated, but we had no snare to trap it. We had no way to provide food for ourselves. We were forsaken in this Desert of Beersheba.

Unable to find a cave for refuge, I made my son lie down under the only shade I could find, a small woeful bush. Weary and worn, my son did not whimper as I left him and hobbled away. I had taken on the shame of ridicule and rejection for my son's innocent life, and for the way we were cast off from our home. But I would not watch him die.

I stumbled on a stone and plummeted to the ground. My leg struck another rock as I fell, and pain poured through my limb. I did not cry out, but a sob escaped my lips. When the lashing ache receded, my eyes opened once more to a distant shimmer. But the false vision of water mocked me, and I resisted the desire to run toward the apparition. There would be nothing to drink in these scorched riverbeds and dry canyons.

The vultures cast long shadows upon us and flew in ever tapering rings, sharp-eyed and unwavering in their vile intent, gawking at us as if their beaks were already plucking at our flesh.

My eyes closed and my wretched thoughts settled upon my mistress, the object of our travails. Sarah reigned as queen, beloved among the Hebrews and her husband, and yet she was given to attacks of hostile and spiteful scheming. Without fail, I had done her bidding. As her slave I was told to lie down with her husband, to give him offspring. But when fruit sprang up in my womb, instead of rejoicing, my mistress mistreated me. I was repaid evil for good. When I gave birth, I became like a corrupt and wild vine in her garden—she was intent on plucking me out!

In Sarah's old age, when God's promise was fulfilled and he'd given her a son, the look of loathing soon shadowed her countenance when she gazed at me. In her eyes I was the winged pestilence on the sweet grapes of her good fortune. With Isaac as her offspring, my own beloved Ishmael lost his place of honor and I, the respect I had yearned for since leaving my homeland. The young and dutiful Isaac would replace my son in every way, including becoming the heir of my master's land and animals.

I did not design to stir up derision in our household, and yet once Isaac was born I became a foreigner, and once again, a slave. A stranger in a strange land. My name befits my plight, for it means "stranger."

Who can save this Egyptian and her son from death? Even the heavens have gone dim. The God of my master has gone silent. And yet the very meaning of Ishmael is "God hears."

> *Once Isaac was born I became a foreigner, and once again, a slave. A stranger in a strange land.*

As a jar of water is poured out, so are our lives poured out in this desolate place. I could hear the mournful lament of my son, and the sound of it severed my heart in two. I tore at my dark tunic and my Egyptian collar—the last testimony of my birthplace—and I covered myself in dirt. The dust rose and coiled in the wind. I shut my eyes tight and felt tears carving paths down my sunburnt cheeks.

"What is the matter, Hagar? Do not be afraid; God has heard the boy crying as he lies there."

What was this voice from the clouds—an angel sent from the God of my master? Or just a dream?

"Lift the boy up and take him by the hand," the voice commanded, "for I will make him into a great nation."

And then as if a veil lifted from my eyes, I saw a well that I had not seen before. So, I did as the angel commanded. I lifted the boy up and took him by the hand. I filled the skin with water and gave him a drink.

Praise to my God. He fails not, for he saw this stranger and had compassion. Alone and abandoned no more, we would surely not die in the desert that day.

The Story from God's Word
Genesis 21:14-20

Early the next morning Abraham took some food and a skin of water and gave them to Hagar. He set them on her shoulders and then sent her off with the boy. She went on her way and wandered in the Desert of Beersheba.

When the water in the skin was gone, she put the boy under one of the bushes. Then she went off and sat down about a bowshot away, for she thought, "I cannot watch the boy die." And as she sat there, she began to sob.

God heard the boy crying, and the angel of God called to Hagar from heaven and said to her, "What is the matter, Hagar? Do not be afraid; God has heard the boy crying as he lies there. Lift the boy up and take him by the hand, for I will make him into a great nation."

Then God opened her eyes and she saw a well of water. So she went and filled the skin with water and gave the boy a drink.

God was with the boy as he grew up. He lived in the desert and became an archer.

THE STORY—FROM THEN TO NOW

Because we're not used to the inner workings of polygamy or accustomed to building our families through our housekeepers, this Bible story may feel more foreign than others. And yet what is at the root of the conflict and misery of this historical event is something we can all identify with—Sarah's lack of faith and her resolve to jump ahead of God's plan. Because she did not trust God to fulfill his promises, she became entangled with Hagar in a way that was never meant to be.

> *Why do we always want something grander or more theatrical to move us closer to God?*

God had promised Sarah that even in her old age she would bear a son, and that child would father a great nation. Because of her advancing years, she must have thought this miracle was truly inconceivable. Sarah had her maidservant sleep with her husband so that she could have a child through Hagar. Even though this was a common practice at that time, it still reeked of desperation.

I too have been guilty of shoving my rickety rowboat off into dangerous waters because I was getting bored sitting on the bank, waiting for God to send that promised cruise ship. But as I nearly sink in my makeshift plans, I can always see that God really had planned on taking good care of me. If only I'd been more patient.

Remembering God's history of faithfulness, reading God's Word, and spending time listening to his still small voice will keep the world's sway at bay. These three suggestions sound plain, but they are vital to our spiritual health in learning to trust God. Instead of embracing the basics, why do we always want something grander or more theatrical to move us closer to God, to learn to rely on him, to obey his leadings? It reminds me of the eager dieter who wants to know all the glamorous secrets to losing weight but refuses to stick to the essentials, such as eating less and exercising more. We also want these secrets when it comes to knowing God, but we get sluggish in following through with his simple requests.

When we read from his love letter—the Bible—and when we stop our whirling long enough to listen to God, it will help us learn to wait on him. And then we can do what Sarah should have done, which was to wait patiently and with anticipation. We can know with assurance that God is going to create something beautiful, something far more wonderful in our lives than we ever could have imagined.

⊱ THE STORY ⊰
QUESTIONS TO THINK ABOUT

1. What motivated Abraham to send Hagar and Ishmael out into the desert?

2. How do you think Sarah should have handled the situation with Hagar and Ishmael, both before and after Isaac was born?

3. Why do you think God allowed Hagar and her son to wander in the desert?

4. In what kinds of situations did God use angels in the Bible (give a few examples)? How do you think he uses angels in the same way today?

5. It's obvious from the story that God cares about everyone, even the people that men and women choose to despise. How does this truth relate to your own life?

6. Have you ever felt alone and abandoned like Hagar did? How can knowing that God is with you help you at times like those?

TEN

Paul

*They changed their minds and
said he was a god.*
ACTS 28:6

he rain had eased, but the wind left us as cold as the grave.
To warm myself and my companions, I gathered a pile of
brushwood to put on the fire. As I released the branches
into the blaze, a viper, escaping the heat of the flames, coiled
itself around my hand. It bored its teeth into me! The vile beast
dangled in the air, clinging to me with its savage fangs, but I
shook it off into the crackling fire.

A few of our island hosts shrunk back in horror, murmuring
that the adder was the king of snakes and most deadly. One of
them, a pale-eyed young man, assured me I would be dead soon
enough. And to each other they whispered, "This man must be
a murderer; for though he escaped from the sea, the goddess
Justice has not allowed him to live."

I did not laugh, nor did I answer them. I had endured a
shipwreck and prison, hunger and trials, all for the sake of my
blessed Savior, and I would survive this too— this ploy of Satan.

While the men around the fire watched me with vigilant eyes,
waiting for me to swell up and perish from the bite, I feared not
for my well-being. The cold rain had made the fire that much
more welcoming, so I sat down close to the fire and rubbed my

hands in front of the flames, trying to make myself dry and warm.

The tidewater going out to sea and then splashing to the shore was soothing in contrast to the storm we had endured. The memory of the great tempest and our ordeal still remained strong—the erupting fury, the angel's promise, the sinking of our ship, and then the divine miracle.

In spite of the islanders' fear of me, my spirit felt at rest. The coves of Malta were known to be safe harbors, and the blue waters and evergreen hills provided a true haven. Malta, the islanders boasted, was a land of honey. Surely the other men and I would winter here, for navigating the sea had become perilous. My voyage to Rome and my appeal to Caesar would be forced to wait for less treacherous waters.

When the islanders had studied me for some time and were convinced I had suffered no ill effects from the viper, they once again murmured among themselves. Then one of them pronounced, "He is a god."

I would not let them linger in their falsehood. "I am no god," I said, addressing them all. "But I have been saved tonight and on the sea by the one true God."

One of the men brought up his heavy frame and stood before me, challenging me. "What is the name of your god?"

I stood and answered him. "His name is Jesus of Nazareth."

The Story from God's Word
Acts 28:1-6

Once safely on shore, we found out that the island was called Malta. The islanders showed us unusual kindness. They built a fire and welcomed us all because it was raining and cold. Paul gathered a pile of brushwood and, as he put it on the fire, a viper, driven out by the heat, fastened itself on his hand. When the islanders saw the snake hanging from his hand, they said to each other, "This man must be a murderer; for though he escaped from the sea, the goddess Justice has not allowed him to live." But Paul shook the snake off into the fire and suffered no ill effects. The people expected him to swell up or suddenly fall dead; but after waiting a long time and seeing nothing unusual happen to him, they changed their minds and said he was a god.

THE STORY—FROM THEN TO NOW

To endure a shipwreck and then a deadly viper bite seems horrific to say the least, but through Paul's life, he suffered many more trials than these. Satan attacked him at every turn, because Paul was making great strides in furthering the kingdom of God. He was building the church, changing people's lives. He was making an eternal difference, and that is something the Enemy cannot tolerate.

Have you ever felt those attacks, especially when you're doing something that you know is pleasing to God? Something you felt called to do? I have experienced these attacks in a hundred different forms. This spiritual battle is as real as the ground we stand on, and this struggle can be as deadly as the viper that clung to Paul's hand. But thank God we don't have to hide out in our homes, trembling in terror. God has the final say in this world and in our individual lives. He knows the tricks of the Enemy firsthand, since he too had to endure many of them while he walked this earth with us.

> *Have you ever felt those attacks, especially when you're doing something that you know is pleasing to God?*

We can be assured that God is watching over our comings and goings, and that "neither death nor life, neither angels nor demons, neither the present nor the future, nor any powers, neither height nor depth, nor anything else in all creation, will be able to separate us from the love of God that is in Christ Jesus our Lord" (Romans 8:38, 39). And to be wrapped in his love—well, that's always the very best place to be.

❧ THE STORY ☙
QUESTIONS TO THINK ABOUT

1. Paul was shipwrecked on the island of Malta. Why do you think God allowed this frightening episode in Paul's ministry?

2. Paul was bitten by a deadly snake. How did God turn this event around for his glory?

3. After the people on the island saw that Paul suffered no ill effects from the snake bite, they thought he was a god. What does this tell you about the beliefs of this people?

4. Paul's life was riddled with spiritual warfare. In what ways have you felt spiritual warfare?

5. What tools did Paul have to help him claim victories in the spiritual battles he fought? How have you won spiritual battles in your life?

6. In the times you were defeated or delayed by the Enemy, what was one thing that kept you from victory?

7. Paul was not perfect, but he was a great spiritual leader. How can we live more like Paul?

ELEVEN

Ruth

Your people will be my people and
your God my God.

RUTH 1:16

I know the weight of death—the way its serpentine burden coils around one's being. My husband's fever had overtaken him so quickly, so dreadfully. Once we laid his body in the dusty ground, I became a part of the desert with him, dried up with no spring to feed it, thirsty and without hope. The remains of my beloved family mark the land but for a short time, but the grief will stain my spirit forever.

Life begins at birth, and the years meander like a stream. But at times, it dries up too soon—before the water can flow down the hillsides and wander through the valleys, to water the land and bring new life to the earth. So it was with my husband. He was the stream that vanished.

I touched my body and grieved the loss of children—my babies—who would never be born, or run in the barley fields, or grow and have children of their own. I would never know the joy of my womb.

I looked up at Naomi, grieving mother of my husband, and of another son who also had succumbed to the fever. She was already weary in the sun and yet we had only begun our journey toward Bethlehem. I surveyed the load on our donkey and then spoke to Naomi. "There is room for you on our beast. I will carry some of the load. Please. You must rest."

Naomi stared down the road toward Orpah, her other son's wife. "Your sister-in-law is going back to her people and her gods. Go back with her, Ruth. There is still time to join her."

I would never go back.

There on the dusty road, I knelt on the ground in front of my husband's mother and clung to her robes. "Please do not press me to go, to leave you. Where you go I will go, and where you stay I will stay. Your people will be my people and your God my God. Where you die I will die, and there I will be buried. May the Lord deal with me, be it ever so severely, if even death separates you and me."

I looked up at Naomi. Her eyes appeared as dark as twilight, but the lines drawn on her face by worry and sorrow softened for a moment. She looked down the long road leading to her home and sighed. *Was I a burden to her?*

For a long moment, I waited for an answer and prayed for favor. I looked up again, and Naomi gave me a slow nod. "So be it, my daughter." She laid her hand softly on my head.

You will be my mother, Naomi. You will be my home.

"We have little food," she said. "Some barley bread, dried olives, and figs . . . When I went away, my hands were full; now they are empty." She stared down at her weathered and callused palms, and sighed again.

I would never go back.

I put my own hand in one of hers. "Not empty now. We will face the perils on the road together . . . be it hunger, robbers, wild animals, or weariness." I rose from the ground and brushed the dust from my tunic and mantle.

The sun had now toiled its way across the sky to the place where it met the earth. The light was no longer oppressive, no longer a threat. I took the donkey's tether into my hand, and we set off again, side by side, toward Naomi's homeland.

Awe creased my face, and a timid joy settled in my heart. I remembered that Naomi had spoken of a relative—a man named Boaz—and I wondered what hope he might offer us . . .

THE STORY FROM GOD'S WORD
RUTH 1:14-19

Then Orpah kissed her mother-in-law goodbye, but Ruth clung to her.

"Look," said Naomi, "your sister-in-law is going back to her people and her gods. Go back with her."

But Ruth replied, "Don't urge me to leave you or to turn back from you. Where you go I will go, and where you stay I will stay. Your people will be my people and your God my God. Where you die I will die, and there I will be buried. May the Lord deal with me, be it ever so severely, if even death separates you and me." When Naomi realized that Ruth was determined to go with her, she stopped urging her.

So the two women went on until they came to Bethlehem.

THE STORY—FROM THEN TO NOW

Loyalty—it's a word that's gone out of vogue in recent years. As our society embraces a more transitory, short-attention, throwaway lifestyle, relationships don't seem to be as deeply cherished as in earlier years. Concepts such as steadfastness and devotion and fidelity don't seem to make it into everyday conversation anymore, let alone our lives. In fact, those values seem as old-fashioned as sitting out on the porch to watch the fireflies.

I have a close friend named Brenda—that's her real name, by the way—who has clung to me for almost twenty years. She has been what Anne of Green Gables called her friend Diana Barry—a bosom friend and kindred spirit. In spite of my occasional lapses in calling Brenda, my failing to have her over for coffee, and my forgetting to pray for her, she remains steadfast.

Brenda has seen me at my worst. Yes, she's seen the dark side of Anita Higman, and incredibly, she still loves me. Brenda is a dedicated friend like Ruth was to Naomi. She is like the Proverbs 18:24 friend—"one who sticks closer than a brother." There are rewards for this kind of commitment—it pleases God.

The biblical account of Ruth and Naomi paints a picture of the falling away of the Israelites and their homecoming back into God's favor. But I especially love the literal story here. Boaz told Ruth how impressed he was with her faithfulness toward Naomi. He even referred to her as noble. Boaz must have thought, if Ruth could be that committed to her mother-in-law, then she would surely be a devoted wife and mother. In the end, Ruth did marry Boaz. And Naomi went from being empty and bitter to having renewed life, and arms filled with her sweet grandson.

I absolutely love this happily-ever-after story.

In fact, Ruth the Moabite is rewarded in another way, since she becomes not only the great-grandmother to Israel's King David, but she is placed in the lineage of Jesus! This miraculous story all began with a humble concept, but a very powerful and honorable one—*loyalty*.

❧ THE STORY ❧
QUESTIONS TO THINK ABOUT

1. One of the themes of the book of Ruth is the deep loyalty and friendship that can form between women. Who are some of the women in your life who have been like beloved sisters to you? What makes these women so special to you?

2. What does it take to make a friendship last a lifetime?

3. What were some of the bonds that held Ruth and Naomi together?

4. How might life have been harder for either one of them if they had gone their separate ways?

5. Do you think these kinds of long-term friendships please God? Why?

6. How do you think people in general view loyalty today?

7. What benefits come from living a life of faithfulness to family and friends?

TWELVE

The Woman Who Anointed His Feet

Then Jesus said to her,
"Your sins are forgiven."
LUKE 7:48

My name is Abeda, and it means "one who worships." That is why on this starry night I sought out a man they claim is the long-awaited Messiah—the holy one named Jesus.

On entering the room where my Lord ate his supper, I felt a burst of understanding take hold of me. A sacred glow bathed the room like silvery waters sprinkling down from heaven. I knew who Jesus was—there could be no doubt—he was the anointed one. I stood in the shadows just beyond the crowd of men who reclined at the table. My Lord dipped his bread into the copper dish of lentil stew and ate it. As he was eating, he turned toward me. Even though I'd made not a sound, his full attention now rested on my presence.

I lowered my eyes, tears of shame stained my cheeks. I hurried toward him and dropped to my knees. Quiet sobs racked my body as one by one my sins returned to me. I felt every transgression, like a dagger piercing me. I knew every scene of iniquity as if it were lived once again in shame. And yet with each memory came a tender mercy. With each thought came a new breath. Of liberation—a freedom I had never felt before.

Purity like that of a dove without blemish replaced the soiled remnant of my soul. My mark of defilement was blotted out, washed clean. This undeserved innocence brought a fresh flow of tears, but this time my weeping came from a glad heart.

I let down my hair and wiped his feet with my tresses, and with gentle affection, kissed his feet again and again. Gasps could be heard around the room, but I paid little heed to anyone's murmuring protests. Yet I felt their eyes on me, staring at me with disdain.

I picked up my vial of perfume and turned the neck, breaking the wax seal. The fragrance filled the room, sweetening the air. The precious ointment—though infused with the most lovely scents of the earth—could never hold as much beauty as the One whom I adored. The aroma, warm and rich, was the scent of royalty. Fit for kings. Fit for my Savior.

I poured the nard on my Lord's feet as I poured out my thanksgiving, my love for the Christ. I dared to raise my eyes to look into his. I knew the words he would say to me, even though nothing but love passed between us. He would say that the aroma of repentance was as sweet to him as the world's most costly nard, but I had brought both. My heart rejoiced at his pleasure in my gifts. And my spirit sang with my rightness before God and man—a sacred gift that only Jesus could offer.

When Simon, the Pharisee, saw what I had done, I knew he would judge me severely. "If this so-called prophet only knew who was touching him! We all know what kind of woman this is."

Simon's words were uttered under his breath, but they had reached my ears, and those of my Lord. Jesus turned his attention to his host. "Simon, I have something to tell you."

"Tell me, teacher," replied Simon.

"Two people owed money to a certain moneylender. One owed him five hundred denarii, and the other fifty. Neither of them had the money to pay him back, so he forgave the debts of both. Now which of them will love him more?"

Simon replied, "I suppose the one who had the bigger debt forgiven."

"You have judged correctly," Jesus said.

> *And yet with each memory came a tender mercy. With each thought came a new breath.*

Then he turned toward the woman and said to Simon, "Do you see this woman? I came into your house. You did not give me any water for my feet, but she wet my feet with her tears and wiped them with her hair. You did not give me a kiss, but this woman, from the time I entered, has not stopped kissing my feet. You did not put oil on my head, but she has poured perfume on my feet. Therefore, I tell you, her many sins have been forgiven—as her great love has shown. But whoever has been forgiven little loves little."

Then Jesus said to me, "Your sins are forgiven."

THE STORY FROM GOD'S WORD
LUKE 7:36-38; 47-50

When one of the Pharisees invited Jesus to have dinner with him, he went to the Pharisee's house and reclined at the table. A woman in that town who lived a sinful life learned that Jesus was eating at the Pharisee's house, so she came there with an alabaster jar of perfume. As she stood behind him at his feet weeping, she began to wet his feet with her tears. Then she wiped them with her hair, kissed them and poured perfume on them.

"Therefore, I tell you, her many sins have been forgiven—as her great love has shown. But whoever has been forgiven little loves little."

Then Jesus said to her, "Your sins are forgiven."

The other guests began to say among themselves, "Who is this who even forgives sins?"

Jesus said to the woman, "Your faith has saved you; go in peace."

THE STORY—FROM THEN TO NOW

Recently, when I reread this Bible account about the woman who anointed Jesus' feet with perfume, I broke down in tears. I loved the exquisite way the story revealed the tender affections that God has for humanity. Jesus didn't dwell on the woman's sins of the past; he was more interested in her repentant spirit of the present. He rewarded her with his forgiveness, his praise in front of the Pharisee, and his peace that passes all understanding. In John 3:17 it says that Jesus came not to condemn the world, but to save it, and this truth could not be more evident, more poignantly and unforgettably and beautifully displayed, than in this passage.

> *She came without a laundry list of requests,*
> *but with a heart for worship.*

We spend most of our lives begging God for help and healing and gifts of every kind. God does say, "Ask and you shall receive," and yet he longs for more—a relationship with us. With you and me. I think that is what impressed Jesus about this woman—she came with a heart full of love.

Recently, I prayed this prayer—that God would show me how to love him. I've prayed every other kind of prayer, and there is hardly anything I haven't asked for. But I thought, *I would really like to please God, not in a vain attempt to work my way up to heaven, but to thank him for his forgiveness and to enjoy his fellowship more intimately.* Through this story I think Jesus has given us all a lesson on how to love him. The woman showed up at the feet of Jesus with a humble and generous spirit. She came without a laundry list of requests, but with a heart for worship.

She came with devotion and fervor and affection, and because of God's mercy, she left with a miracle.

❧ THE STORY ☙
QUESTIONS TO THINK ABOUT

1. What were the differences between the woman's attitude and the host's mind-set in the way they approached Jesus?

2. The perfume that was poured on the feet of Jesus was expensive. What do you think motivated the woman to be so extravagant? What other extravagant gifts given to Jesus does this remind you of?

3. Some of the most precious gifts given to Jesus were given from people whose paths would seem to be the furthest from following Christ. What lessons do these illustrations give us about our hearts, about grace and judgment, and about what it means to surrender to Christ?

4. Why do you think the woman was weeping?

5. Jesus didn't dwell on the sins of the woman but simply forgave her. Sometimes it's easy for us to spend so much time dwelling on past sins and suffering that we become feeble spiritually, rather than dynamic. How can we avoid that trap?

6. Do you think the woman had a heart for worship? What qualities of worship can we see in what she did and how she did it?

7. Jesus said that whoever has been forgiven little will love little. Have you found that truth to be significant in your own life? How so?

THIRTEEN

Jonah

But you, Lord my God, brought
my life up from the pit.

JONAH 2:6

No man can run from God. There is no hiding place dark enough, no fathom of the sea deep enough that his light cannot pierce. That his will and presence cannot penetrate. Those truths battered my soul as my body writhed inside the belly of a monster.

In the rolling growls of my death chamber, my mind cried out for clarity. Nothing but chaos and fear churned inside me. Hot air seared my flesh, and my vigor drained out of me like the blood from the throat of a slaughtered lamb. Flashes of memory came to me, like sunlight on the waves.

Calamity had befallen me because I ran from God, fleeing his calling on my life. On a ship bound to Tarshish, I had been thrown overboard, and a great fish had swallowed me whole. The whale had saved me from drowning, and yet darkness deeper than night and more frightening than any evil dream engulfed me. The beast's oily insides clung to my body, drawing life from me.

I gouged at the beast with my fists and teeth. The slimy muscles gave way to my touch, but despite the struggle, my body succumbed to a terrible rippling pressure—the weight and horror of being eaten alive!

I moved and breathed inside this living grave. I cried out to the Almighty, my only salvation, my final hope. "While my life is ebbing away, I have remembered you, Lord. My prayers rise to you, to your holy temple. Those who are clinging to worthless idols will turn away from your love for them. But I, with shouts of grateful praise, will sacrifice to you. What I have vowed I will make good. I will say to them, 'Salvation comes from the Lord.'"

I breathed deeply, curled my body up like an infant in the lightless space, and waited for God to deliver me. Or for the beast to consume what was left of me.

Calamity had befallen me because I ran from God.

The lamenting groan of the beast startled me, and then in one swift lunge, my body moved forward. The great fish convulsed and coughed me out of his mouth. I tumbled out onto land, my body rolling high up onto the dry shore. I rested, drenched in thanksgiving.

I turned my head to see the beast that in the watery deep had been my salvation, and very nearly my death. The monster fish did not look at me—the tormenting morsel he had vomited up onto land—but he pitched his tail instead and slid backward, vanishing beyond the waves.

I remembered my vow and the idolatrous nation I was to save from destruction. They did not deserve mercy, and yet I knew I would not fail God again. I would speak the words he ordained. God brought me out to the light, and I would bring his light to the people of Nineveh.

The Story from God's Word

Jonah 2:1-10

From inside the fish Jonah prayed to the Lord his God. He said:
In my distress I called to the Lord, and he answered me.
From deep in the realm of the dead I called for help,

and you listened to my cry.
You hurled me into the depths, into the very heart of the seas,
*   and the currents swirled about me;*
all your waves and breakers swept over me.
I said, 'I have been banished from your sight;
yet I will look again toward your holy temple.'
The engulfing waters threatened me, the deep surrounded me;
*   seaweed was wrapped around my head.*
To the roots of the mountains I sank down;
*   the earth beneath barred me in forever.*
But you, Lord my God, brought my life up from the pit.
When my life was ebbing away, I remembered you, Lord,
and my prayer rose to you, to your holy temple.
Those who cling to worthless idols
*   turn away from God's love for them.*
But I, with shouts of grateful praise, will sacrifice to you.
What I have vowed I will make good.
*   I will say, "Salvation comes from the Lord."*

And the Lord commanded the fish, and it vomited Jonah onto dry land.

THE STORY—FROM THEN TO NOW

Humans are good at hiding. Ever since Adam and Eve hid from God because of their sin, we have been perfecting the art of secreting ourselves away from our Creator.

In Jonah's story, that is exactly what he attempted to do—hide from God. But since God is omnipresent, no one has ever been able to succeed in that endeavor, including Jonah. It's futile. And yet, we still try over and over and over, as if the next time we really will achieve such an impossible task. You name it, we're hiding from it—from God's holiness, his will, his people. We're like foolish children who stand covered in a bed sheet, thinking we are completely invisible.

In my own life, one good example of running from God is when I try to pray with my husband after we've had an unresolved quarrel. It feels very uncomfortable to come before God as if nothing is wrong, when in truth we've not forgiven each other. Why is that? Because the imprint of God on our souls reminds us that we are to seek understanding and peace, not discord and strife. If reconciliation hasn't happened with my husband, the last thing my pride wants to do is humble myself, kneel before God, and pray with him. So, in essence, I am running from what is good and right; I am hiding from God.

How do we fix this universal problem? One way to begin is to acknowledge our moral insufficiencies and confess that we've been running. It seems in Jonah's case, he may have thought he was too righteous to preach to the pagans in Nineveh. But God thought otherwise and intervened, helping Jonah to see the error of his ways. I pray we can all run from our pride rather than from the One who only wants what is good and holy and lovely. Life will be so much more like heaven when we all live that exquisite truth.

⊁ THE STORY ⊱
QUESTIONS TO THINK ABOUT

1. Jonah tried to hide from God. We all know that's impossible, and yet we've all been guilty of attempting it. Give an example of a time when you tried to flee from God. How did it turn out?

2. What do you think the imagery of this dramatic event— Jonah inside the stomach of a mammoth fish—is meant to tell us about God? What does it tell us about Jonah?

3. Jonah finally obeyed God and became a prophet to the Ninevites, but he became angry when the people listened to his preaching and repented. Have you ever felt that the free gift of grace was given a little too freely (to someone else, of course)? Describe that situation. Why did you feel that way?

4. It's clear from this Bible story that Jonah got himself into his own mess—he ran from the job God had for him to an even more dangerous and more stressful circumstance. Describe a time when you were afraid of or annoyed by the task God had placed in front of you, and yet did it anyway. What happened? Did you feel like God partnered with you in your work? If so, how?

5. Who can you more closely relate to in the story—Jonah or the Ninevites? Explain your answer.

6. In Jonah's prayer he says, "You listened to my cry. You hurled me into the depths." What does this say to you about the ways God answers our prayers?

FOURTEEN

Martha

But Martha was distracted by all the
preparations that had to be made.
Luke 10:40

⟨flourish⟩

I punched the mound of dough again as I thought of my sister, Mary, flaunting her most practiced art—resting! She was much more accomplished at being sleepy and slothful than being occupied with real work. *Clank.* I clapped the lid back on the pot of lentil soup. While I labored in front of the hot coals, baking the bread and stirring the pot, Mary idled at the foot of Jesus, trying to understand the thoughts of man. Attempting what was not meant for a woman—to be the student of a rabbi. Only in a dream might a woman learn in such a way. Surely Jesus did not approve of my sister's unnatural thirst for knowledge. Surely he would align himself with my view—that Mary must devote herself to preparing the supper and serving our guests.

I wiped the flour from my hands and went to Jesus, "Lord, don't you care that my sister has left me to do the work by myself? Tell her to help me!" When I saw the look of displeasure on my Lord's face, I withered, knowing I should not have lifted my voice in anger. "But Lord, we are almost out of flour, and someone must gather more brambles from the hillsides for the fire."

His eyes pierced mine, but they were not unkind or angry.

"Martha, Martha," the Lord said to me, "you are worried and upset about many things, but few things are needed . . . or indeed only one. Mary has chosen what is better, and it will not be taken away from her."

I said no more, for I had said more than wisdom would allow. I was stunned by his words. *Few things? Few?* With the soup and the bread and the cleaning and the table to be laid out and the floor to be swept and the animals to be attended to and . . . *Or indeed only one? What could he possibly mean?*

My eyes ran about the room, seeing all that needed done. Then Jesus began speaking to Mary again. I watched Mary's face—filled with joy. Even as a young girl, my sister had always loved what was sacred and wise. While I had sought to gain accomplishments and the praise of those who admired my hospitality, she had chosen quieter paths, and spent much time listening to teachers and readings of Scripture.

Perhaps in seeking to do good, I had failed to remember all that *was* good, all that was holy. But I was not without the will to change. Kneeling before Jesus, I ignored the mess around me and smoothed the lines in my forehead. Jesus reached down and touched the crown of my head. Warmth came through me like sunlight filtering through the leaves. Like yeast through dough. The supper meal paled in importance to what was before me, *who* was before me—the food of heaven, the bread of life. The living manna of our ancestors! Yes, indeed only One was needed. Only One, for life now and forever—Jesus.

The Story from God's Word
Luke 10:38-42

As Jesus and his disciples were on their way, he came to a village where a woman named Martha opened her home to him. She had a sister called Mary, who sat at the Lord's feet listening to what he said. But Martha was distracted by all the preparations that had to be made. She came to him and asked, "Lord, don't you care that my sister has left me to do the work by myself? Tell her to help me!"

"Martha, Martha," the Lord answered, "you are worried and

upset about many things, but few things are needed—or indeed only one. Mary has chosen what is better, and it will not be taken away from her."

THE STORY—FROM THEN TO NOW

I can relate to Martha's story very well—too well—since I am a woman of busyness. My family would say that is no exaggeration. I can sit and relax for a few minutes, but before long my hands start to fidget. I want to create something, clean something, or give somebody something to eat! I am a modern-day Martha. I'm distracted easily by, well, everything. For instance, when I pray, my mind may not wander to the brambles that need to be gathered for the fire, but I may think about the meat I need to buy at the store for the pasta sauce.

There's nothing wrong with the things that Martha and I get sidetracked with, but it's all about priorities. Sometimes even the most virtuous things in life can be a distraction—it's easy to use the excuse that we are chasing after what is good and wholesome. But even good books cannot replace God's Word, and even the most eloquent sermons cannot replace that still small voice of God. Satan would like nothing better than to keep us so focused on the gnats flying around our heads that we don't see God's sustaining fruit right in front of us.

> *Sometimes even the most virtuous things in life can be a distraction.*

But the good news is that even though many of us are like Martha, we are really Mary wannabes! The transformation can be as easy as knowing the secret to friendship. If I've met someone new and want her to be my friend, I'll need to spend time with her. It's the same way to build a relationship with Jesus. He's waiting for us to dust the flour of life off our hands, sit at his feet, and feel his holy touch on our lives.

✴ THE STORY ✴
QUESTIONS TO THINK ABOUT

1. In the story of Mary and Martha, which character can you relate to more, and why?

2. Martha was intent on being a good hostess and making sure her guests had plenty of food. Why wasn't she commended at all for her good intentions and hard work?

3. Is there ever an instance when practical work is more important than spiritual concerns? Explain.

4. What do you think Jesus was saying to Mary that was so important? What does each woman's interaction with Jesus possibly tell us about the state of her heart and what she needed from the Lord?

5. It's so easy to get sidetracked in life, away from Christ. What keeps you from your daily quiet time with the Lord—that is, what keeps you from sitting at the foot of Jesus, listening to what he has to say to you?

6. When Martha rebuked her sister for not helping with the dinner preparations, Jesus said to Martha, "you are worried and upset about many things, but few things are needed—or indeed only one." What was the one thing that Jesus was talking about?

FIFTEEN

Rahab

So they went and entered the house of a
prostitute named Rahab and stayed there.

JOSHUA 2:1

I once saw a man snare a bird without killing it. The man thrust the winged creature into a cage. It fluttered with life, but since it fought for its freedom by beating itself against the iron bars, its heart weakened, its wings broke, and blood stained its breast.

I am Rahab, the bird, and Jericho is my cage.

I looked out over the countryside from my dwelling up on the city wall. The Jordan River, the mountains, and the many sycamores and date palms that adorned the landscape stretched out before me. If God would bring favor to my plan, I would take flight and be free, not from this fertile land, this fruitful plain of milk and honey; but I would escape the evil that coursed through Jericho like the plagues of Egypt. The surrender of life, of babes sacrificed as the "firstfruits" gifts to Baal—the Lord of Rain and Dew—was surely witnessed by the God of the Hebrews. Our slaughter of innocent life, the bloodshed, must be an abomination to him and must ascend to the heavens like the stench of an open grave.

A hasty knock came at my door, and I shuddered. I drew tight the girdle around my waist and then arranged my cap. Someday soon I hoped to put away my raiment of scarlet, my painted eyes, and the jingling of my jewelry, but not tonight. Not yet. Because I had given myself to the lustful pleasures of the wealthy merchants, I had defiled my body—my temple was swathed in the foul dregs of Jericho. But no more would I remain ensnared in such depravity. Perhaps my plot to break free from my life of sin would work. *God in heaven, may it be so!*

I unbolted the latch on the door, knowing who might call at such a late hour and what my words would be. Two soldiers of the king—one a man, another a giant from the brood of Anak—stood in my inner hallway. The giant, more than five cubits tall, loomed above the other soldier. I looked away from the shiny, unblinking eyes of the giant. I had seen these hulking fiends before, but on this night the sight of him spilled terror through my heart.

Without greeting me, the other soldier said, "We know that two Israelite men have come to you—they have come to spy out the whole land. Bring them out to us. With haste, woman!"

I answered the soldier, "Yes, the men came to me, but I did not know where they had come from. At dusk, when it was time to close the city gate, they left."

I stayed fixed in my lie, even though my legs quaked under my tunic. The two men the soldiers spoke of rested just above me on the roof, hidden by my own hand under bundles of flax. They were not musicians or farmers or priests. They were indeed spies. I was now a traitor to my kingdom, but I would not alter my course. I had come to know the one true God, and he would surely save me and my family because of the kindness I had shown to the two Israelites.

The soldier's gaze ravaged me, and I clutched the scarlet cord wrapped around my waist. His words mocked me. "You are no more than a harlot, so for you, lies flow like the Jordan."

"My words are truth." I lifted my chin to the soldier, and then gaped at the giant, not turning away from the shiny, unblinking eyes. "I don't know which way they went. Go after them quickly. You may catch up with them." With a grunt of resignation, the soldiers departed, and I shut the door.

God would conquer the Canaanites, for they were melting in fear. They would scatter just as the rodents did when driven out of the dark corners of the city by the lamplight. The fortified walls of Jericho could never hold against the mighty forces of God.

> *I was now a traitor to my kingdom,*
> *but I would not alter my course.*

I climbed the stone stairs and made my way up to the roof to ready my guests for their escape. The stars had come to light the way in the hours of darkness, to hail the night—when the Lord of all would change the fortunes and the course of men. I murmured to the cool night air, "Yes, I am the bird, but Jericho will no longer be my cage."

Soon, very soon, I would be set free. *Praise to the God of the Israelites, for the Lord my God is God in heaven above and on the earth below!*

THE STORY FROM GOD'S WORD

JOSHUA 2:1-7

Then Joshua son of Nun secretly sent two spies from Shittim. "Go, look over the land," he said, "especially Jericho." So they went and entered the house of a prostitute named Rahab and stayed there.

The king of Jericho was told, "Look, some of the Israelites have come here tonight to spy out the land." So the king of Jericho sent this message to Rahab: "Bring out the men who came to you and entered your house, because they have come to spy out the whole land."

But the woman had taken the two men and hidden them. She said, "Yes, the men came to me, but I did not know where they had come from. At dusk, when it was time to close the city gate, they left. I don't know which way they went. Go after them quickly. You may catch up with them." (But she had taken them up to the roof and hidden them under the stalks of flax she had laid out on the roof.)

So the men set out in pursuit of the spies on the road that leads to the fords of the Jordan, and as soon as the pursuers had gone out, the gate was shut.

The Story—from Then to Now

The definition of risk is the possibility of something going awry. Being alive involves a certain amount of risk—on the level of exposing bare legs in a room filled with mosquitoes. You will get bitten. Even staying at home can be hazardous—most accidents happen in the home. It makes me wonder how I should live. How many risks am I willing to take? I may decide not to eat raw fish at a sushi bar. That's fine. I may not want to go spelunking or bungee jumping. No problem. But what about spiritual risks? It's not as easy for a Christian to walk away from something that's immoral but popular in the culture—especially when it seems that everyone else insists it's a good thing.

The risk Rahab took for God put her life in jeopardy. She could no longer embrace the evil deeds that she saw around her—deeds that she had once participated in. She could sense in her spirit that the Israelite God was *the* God—he was the great "I Am," the God over heaven and earth—and she was willing to risk everything to do what she thought was right and to save herself and her family.

How many risks am I willing to take?

In the end, Rahab and her clan were indeed spared when the city of Jericho was destroyed. What would I do if presented with the same situation? When faced with matters of faith, do I always take a stand for Christ, for the sake of righteousness and justice, even if it means loss or humiliation or peril? I pray that God will give us the strength to be as daring and committed and unflappable as Rahab!

✦ THE STORY ✦
QUESTIONS TO THINK ABOUT

1. Rahab risked everything, including her life, to help the Israelite spies with their mission. What was Rahab's motivation in doing this?

2. What message do you think God is sending us by letting us see the lowly prostitute become the heroine in this story?

3. Do you think that God can use anyone for his purposes and glory, no matter who they are or what they've done? Why or why not?

4. Do you take spiritual risks for the kingdom of God? Give several examples.

5. Has God taken a risk on us? Explain your answer.

SIXTEEN

Eve

Then the eyes of both of them were opened,
and they realized they were naked.
GENESIS 3:7

As Adam and I gathered greens and wild plums for our noonday meal, a slithery movement in the grass captured my attention. I stared at the earth to see what it was. A serpent beast, with eyes like currants and skin the color of honey, peered up at me. Then he hid behind a cluster of poppies, as if to tease me. I followed the creature as he darted here and there. Thinking it a game, I allowed myself to be drawn deeper into the garden and farther away from my love.

Soon I realized that our amusement had brought me to a fertile hill in the heart of Eden. I knew the very place I had been taken.

I gazed into the sinewy arms of the tree of the knowledge of good and evil. I had seen it from a distance only, but now that I stood beneath its branches, the tree seemed to summon me to take a closer look. I marveled at the immensity of it. Its beauty was so exotic, I felt heady and light and began to sing under its mighty wings. Amidst my merry chants, shadows crossed my thoughts like clouds covering the sun. For the first time, I questioned my existence—my life in the garden. What lay beyond Eden? Beyond my own understanding?

The breeze made a sly whisper through the blousy leaves. The fruit on every branch appeared like none other—rosy in hue, voluptuous in shape, and spicy in aroma. The way the dew on their skin caught the light made them even more irresistible. Such rich, ripe fruit and oh! How they aroused my senses!

"I will call the fruit *lushifer*." But the moment I had given the fruit its name, a murmuring arose from among the leaves, "Did God really say, 'You must not eat from any tree in the garden?'"

Had the tree been given speech as well as fruit?

I turned my full attention to the fruit now and ran my tongue over my fingers. The lushifer looked eager to be touched, like an impatient lover, longing for someone to taste its sweetness. Almost against my will, my hand reached up to touch it, but I drew back before my fingers caressed its fern-soft flesh.

I studied the splendid thing—the only fruit forbidden in all of Eden. The lushifer did not teem with bitterness and death as I had imagined. It appeared . . . desirable.

I had never once disobeyed our Creator, for I loved him. But to gaze upon the beauty of the fruit did no harm. Perhaps I would slip away from Adam again tomorrow and return to the forbidden place. As I backed away to leave, I heard a hiss. It was not the air that stirred, but the creature that had brought me to the tree. He'd wound himself around the belly of the tree and gazed at me, as if to say, "Here am I, a creature of God. I am in this tree and yet not dead!"

The serpent vanished behind the leaves. I took a step closer. I had seen glimpses of this serpent beast in the wild long before we shared our morning game. He was not like the other animals, since he did not forage for food, but merely watched. He was a creature of mystery and of fierce grandeur, and yet on this day he was something more. Never had I been so inquisitive about his presence, never so entranced by him. He edged out onto a branch—his head suspended near my own—and uttered in a voice most pleasing to my ears, "Surely you will not die."

I answered the serpent from the words I had committed to memory: "We may eat fruit from the trees in the garden, but

God did say, 'You must not eat fruit from the tree that is in the middle of the garden, and you must not touch it, or you will die.'"

The beast murmured, "God knows that when you eat from it your eyes will be opened, and you will be like God, knowing good and evil." He dipped his head behind another lushifer. I came closer to hear his whispers, but he said no more. Perhaps when evening comes I should speak to God about my thoughts, about my yearning to taste the lushifer. Surely the Creator of all things would understand my desire for knowledge and wisdom.

Almost bowing, I leaned toward the tree once more, looking for the creature. "Where did you go?"

I could hear Adam beckoning me. I did not give him a happy shout back as I always did, but waited for him to find me. He came from the other side of the tree, and we saw each other, but not fully. A lushifer dangled between us, sighing with promises. Yes, to be wise like God—what could be more pure and good? Adam and I would no longer walk with God in the evenings— we would *be* gods! With this fruit I could have the wisdom I needed to be the perfect helper to Adam.

> *Never had I been so inquisitive about his presence, never so entranced by him.*

My hand came so near the fruit that it grazed the skin of the lushifer. This new knowledge, this choice, was fated from the beginning. I could see this now. My eyes already opened to the truth—the truth that God had hidden from me. One by one my fingers enfolded and embraced the juicy flesh. I squeezed, letting the nectar drip from its body. Before I could calm my delirium or talk to Adam about the fruit, I plucked it from the branch, drew it to my lips, and took a bite.

Adam walked up to me, and I handed him the lushifer. He was not angry at me, but quiet and curious about what I had done. He raised the fruit up to the sunlight and turned it in his palm. Juice trickled down his arm. Finally, without speaking, he gave me an earnest nod, lowered the lushifer to his mouth, and took a bite.

Even as I watched Adam consume the fruit, already I felt shaken from my guileless perch—that place of paradisaical harmony. I could see what was never seen before. Terrible secrets and strange pangs of feeling closed me in like a night without stars. Without God. I could not fathom the darkness. Life and love and time altered forever in that moment. My moment— the moment of Eve—and now of Adam.

I could see the change in the eyes of my beloved. The guileless twinkle that I adored was now replaced with an awareness that burned without restraint. We were still one body, but just as the loftiest branches were harder to reach, a distance grew between us. It too I could not measure.

I looked for the serpent, but the creature had disappeared from the tree.

I beheld our world with new eyes, yes. But the serpent had lied. I was not a god. I looked down at my body, which no longer felt limitless, like the birds of the sky. My very skin felt dry and attached to the earth, like dust under my feet.

And for the first time, I saw it—I was naked.

The Story from God's Word

Genesis 3:1-7

Now the serpent was more crafty than any of the wild animals the Lord God had made. He said to the woman, "Did God really say, 'You must not eat from any tree in the garden'?"

The woman said to the serpent, "We may eat fruit from the trees in the garden, but God did say, 'You must not eat fruit from the tree that is in the middle of the garden, and you must not touch it, or you will die.'"

"You will not certainly die," the serpent said to the woman. "For God knows that when you eat from it your eyes will be opened, and you will be like God, knowing good and evil."

When the woman saw that the fruit of the tree was good for food and pleasing to the eye, and also desirable for gaining wisdom, she took some and ate it. She also gave some to her husband, who was with her, and he ate it. Then the eyes of both of them were opened, and they realized they were naked; so they sewed fig leaves together and made coverings for themselves.

THE STORY—FROM THEN TO NOW

To eat a piece of fruit is such a natural thing to do, and yet for Adam and Eve in the Garden of Eden, eating the fruit of that particular tree had monumental significance. The Creator had given earth's first couple a glorious garden, which met all their needs. God only asked that they not eat from the tree of the knowledge of good and evil. This command wasn't issued to torture his creation, but to give them free will. Only within the gift of choice could there be a relationship between the Creator and mankind. Otherwise we would be no more than animated clay figures that talk and move but have no real heart.

> *Even for Christians, the tasty morsel of "I'm in control of my own destiny" is tempting.*

Adam and Eve's free will allowed them to choose to believe the serpent's enticement over remaining obedient to God. The serpent's temptation—which was to become like gods—was so tantalizing to Adam and Eve that they relinquished their intimate fellowship with the only God to chase after this vain imagining and fantastical lie. But their defiance had monstrous consequences and brought destruction on all creation.

Satan, in his ageless battle to usurp God's throne, still uses the same seductive ploy today. Many cults and other religions tout the same empty promise—to *become* a god rather than have a relationship with the one true God. And that lie is still as deadly to our souls as it was in Eden.

Even for Christians, the tasty morsel of "I'm in control of my own destiny" is tempting. Every time we get ahead of God's will or go against what we know is right in his eyes, we are touching and tasting that forbidden fruit all over again. We are chasing the lie.

God did make us in his image, but he never meant for us to *be* God. Can we perform miracles? Did we lay the earth's foundations or set the stars in the sky? We aren't even worthy to be his creatures, since we have scrawled our sins all over his perfect imprint. In truth, we have become an ungrateful and inglorious creation.

But there is hope! In Christ, we can recognize Satan's lies. When we come to Christ—that is, letting go of our prideful attitudes and our desires for ascendency—he returns to us part of a paradise lost. He gives us that intimate fellowship with God—those walks and talks with him in the cool of the day.

All we have to do is ask.

✺ THE STORY ✺
QUESTIONS TO THINK ABOUT

1. Why do you think it was necessary for God to have a tree in the Garden of Eden that was off-limits to his creation?

2. Why do you think God allowed the serpent (Satan) to have free reign in the garden?

3. If you had been presented with the same temptations in Eden as Adam and Eve, do you think you could have suppressed the urge to taste the forbidden fruit? Why or why not?

4. When the Serpent was tempting Eve, he said, "You will not certainly die. For God knows that when you eat from it your eyes will be opened, and you will be like God, knowing good and evil." Is that temptation still alive and well today? What various forms does it take?

5. Humans seem to never be satisfied with what is holy and beautiful. We always have to be reaching for more. What do you think this tells us about humanity and the world we live in?

6. What specific qualities that are common to women do you think might have played a part in Eve's deception? Have you noticed any of these traits in yourself?

7. What might the world have looked like if Adam and Eve hadn't eaten from the tree of the knowledge of good and evil?

SEVENTEEN

Thomas

Reach out your hand and put it into my side.
Stop doubting and believe.

JOHN 20:27

No one ever survived Golgotha. The cross was the most brutal of punishments ever to be endured. Jesus was dead. His tomb was sealed. *All is lost.*

Yes, I had seen the Christ heal the sick, feed the hungry, and raise the dead, and yet I could not imagine how he could restore his own life after such injury, after such foul decay.

I gazed around at my brothers. The desolate grief and feverish desire to see our Lord alive again had made them weak in their minds. I feared they had conjured up a ghost or seen a man who merely resembled our Lord.

Talk as blustery as winter's wind erupted from the sons of thunder who sat next to me. They stole me from my contemplations, and yet nothing could dispel my doubts about the Christ. Not until I saw him for myself.

Then a sight—a human form—manifested itself inside the house where we stayed! The man, a stranger, had come through the door, and yet it was locked! *What trickery of the eyes was this?*

The stranger stepped toward us and said, "Peace be with you!"

Then the man, who now seemed familiar, turned to me and said, "Put your finger here; see my hands. Reach out your hand and put it into my side. Stop doubting and believe."

Could it be my Lord?

Obeying almost without thinking, I touched his hands and saw the marks where the nails had been. I placed my hand on his side, and felt the scar from the spear that had pierced him, where blood and water had flowed from his body. The man was indeed Jesus, and he was among the living again! Why had I doubted? His life, his ministry, his countless miracles, had been more than enough proof of his Lordship.

Shame washed over me, drenching me, like a great wave on the shore. "My Lord and my God!"

I knelt before him. *Forgive my doubts.*

Then Jesus said to me, "Because you have seen me, you have believed; blessed are those who have not seen and yet have believed."

The Story from God's Word

John 20:24-29

Now Thomas (also known as Didymus), one of the Twelve, was not with the disciples when Jesus came. So the other disciples told him, "We have seen the Lord!"

But he said to them, "Unless I see the nail marks in his hands and put my finger where the nails were, and put my hand into his side, I will not believe."

A week later his disciples were in the house again, and Thomas was with them. Though the doors were locked, Jesus came and stood among them and said, "Peace be with you!" Then he said to Thomas, "Put your finger here; see my hands. Reach out your hand and put it into my side. Stop doubting and believe."

Thomas said to him, "My Lord and my God!"

Then Jesus told him, "Because you have seen me, you have believed; blessed are those who have not seen and yet have believed."

THE STORY—FROM THEN TO NOW

To doubt God is part of the fallen human experience. To doubt doesn't mean we've abandoned our faith. When Jesus questioned the faith of a father whose boy was demon-possessed, the father exclaimed, "I believe. Help my unbelief!" That is one of my life prayers. I want to have an abundant and usable faith, one that can move molehills as well as mountains. Jesus promises us that if we ask we shall receive, and asking for more faith would surely be considered a selfless and pleasing request.

But after we've received the gift of faith, the undertow of doubts can still take us down when life weakens our spirits with wave after wave of calamity. Even without major adversities, the relentless wear and tear of daily life can make even the most faithful stumble sometimes. The Bible is full of characters who doubted God, Abraham being one of the most prominent. He showed signs of vacillations and fears and uncertainties, even though he was considered a righteous man and a spiritual patriarch!

> *The relentless wear and tear of daily life can make even the most faithful stumble sometimes.*

Perhaps it's best not to run from doubts when they come but, with a prayerful attitude, to confront them head-on. Doubts can make us like the grapevine that searches for, finds, and stretches toward the sunlight. The vine can then grow into all it was meant to be—a vine full of beauty, and one that produces much good fruit.

❧ THE STORY ❧
QUESTIONS TO THINK ABOUT

1. When the disciples were gathered, Jesus came through the door, even though it was locked. How do you think Thomas felt when he realized that the disciples had been right and that Jesus really had risen from the dead?

2. Jesus had done countless miracles during his ministry. What do you think kept Thomas from believing in this instance?

3. We can all too easily sound like Thomas. All we have to do is fill in the blank inside Thomas's speech. We might say to God, "Unless I see _____, I will not believe." What is holding us back from a more perfect faith?

4. Uncertainties are certain to arise in this life. What's the best way to handle the doubts we have about our faith?

5. What part of the story is most significant to you, and why?

6. Then Jesus told Thomas, "Because you have seen me, you have believed; blessed are those who have not seen and yet have believed." May we assume from that verse that if we believe in Jesus, then we are blessed? Explain.

7. Do you remember the day you first believed in Jesus as Lord of your life? Describe your experience.

EIGHTEEN

Esther

*For I and my people have been sold to be
destroyed, killed and annihilated.*

ESTHER 7:4

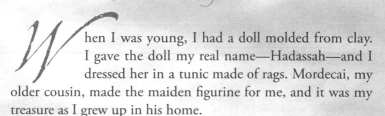

When I was young, I had a doll molded from clay. I gave the doll my real name—Hadassah—and I dressed her in a tunic made of rags. Mordecai, my older cousin, made the maiden figurine for me, and it was my treasure as I grew up in his home.

I smoothed the fine fabric of my royal robes and breathed in the fragrance of myrrh. I had strayed far from my simple beginnings, but my heart remained steadfastly with my people and with Mordecai. I was now queen in the king's palace, but even with my exalted position, I was only moments away from placing myself in great peril. I could no longer ponder the simplicity and shelter of my youth. Mordecai's words, "for such a time as this," pierced through my thoughts.

With an anxious eye I watched the king take pleasure in the banquet I'd created for him—a feast of goat and lamb, of pistachios, apricots, and pomegranates. Aromatic spices permeated the air—saffron, cinnamon, and cloves. He ate and drank with great delight, but I had no appetite for food. Only for justice.

The wine steward refilled the king's goblet, and then King Xerxes turned all his attention to me. He asked, "Queen Esther, what is your petition? It will be given you. What is your request? Even up to half the kingdom, it will be granted."

Haman must be stopped. Lord, my God, speak through me. Grant me mercy. Give me words! With quiet voice and humble posture, I answered the king, "If I have found favor with you, Your Majesty, and if it pleases you, grant me my life—this is my petition. And spare my people—this is my request. For I and my people have been sold to be destroyed, killed and annihilated. If we had merely been sold as male and female slaves, I would have kept quiet, because no such distress would justify disturbing the king."

King Xerxes replied, "Who is he? Where is he—the man who has dared to do such a thing?"

The evil is in our midst. Without addressing Haman or even looking at him, I said, "An adversary and enemy! This vile Haman!"

Haman rose from his couch, terrified at my words.

The king got up in a rage, left his wine and went out into the palace garden.

"I have sealed my fate. I am no more." Haman threw himself on the couch where I reclined. "Save me, Queen Esther!"

"I cannot."

> *I had no appetite for food.*
> *Only for justice.*

Haman's life had been spent exalting himself and conspiring to do wicked deeds with every breath. He would surely die, impaled on the very pole he had constructed for my cousin Mordecai. He would meet with death—the same end, in fact, that he had plotted for all the Jewish people.

Mordecai's words were forged in courage and in truth. I had indeed come to my royal position for such a time as this. God had raised me up to save his people from destruction.

"Hidden" is what the name of Esther means, but from this day on, I will no longer hide. I am Hadassah—a Jewess and an orphan, used by God.

THE STORY FROM GOD'S WORD
ESTHER 7:1-7

So the king and Haman went to Queen Esther's banquet, and as they were drinking wine on the second day, the king again asked, "Queen Esther, what is your petition? It will be given you. What is your request? Even up to half the kingdom, it will be granted."

Then Queen Esther answered, "If I have found favor with you, Your Majesty, and if it pleases you, grant me my life—this is my petition. And spare my people—this is my request. For I and my people have been sold to be destroyed, killed and annihilated. If we had merely been sold as male and female slaves, I would have kept quiet, because no such distress would justify disturbing the king."

King Xerxes asked Queen Esther, "Who is he? Where is he—the man who has dared to do such a thing?"

Esther said, "An adversary and enemy! This vile Haman!"

Then Haman was terrified before the king and queen. The king got up in a rage, left his wine and went out into the palace garden. But Haman, realizing that the king had already decided his fate, stayed behind to beg Queen Esther for his life.

THE STORY—FROM THEN TO NOW

Most of us will never be given the opportunity to do something as dramatic and sacrificial as Esther did—that is, to willingly place our lives in jeopardy to save a nation of people. Esther's story was grandly heroic and led to an awe-inspiring historical event.

But then, all our God-ordained deeds have a heroic quality about them, all may have an impact that is far-reaching. Every cool cup of water given in his name is infused with compassion and lit with glory. Everything, good or evil, curse or blessing, has a powerful ripple effect. Rarely do people get to see how the waves of their actions make it to that distant shore. No matter how small the kindness, no matter how insignificant the effort might look from our earthly vantage point, it will all make a difference. Now and for eternity.

Just as people want their muscles to have flexibility, do our spirits have usability? When the stirring hand of Providence moves, are we willing to be the physical hand that stirs? We can change the world one person at a time with one deed at a time. We all have been born into this world with great purpose . . . for such a time as this.

✤ THE STORY ✤
QUESTIONS TO THINK ABOUT

1. Reading the entire book of Esther will help you get a fuller picture of the way God works with men and women to orchestrate his plans. How have you felt or seen God's guiding hand in your life or in the lives of those around you?

2. After a miraculous series of events, Esther was able to save her people from annihilation. When have you ever seen God working with these same grand brushstrokes today? Describe the situations or series of events.

3. Many people link the quality of bravery with this Bible story. Given the position of women in that culture and at that time, and considering what had happened to Queen Vashti, what do you think was remarkable about what Esther said and did?

4. What do you think God wants us to learn from this story?

5. Do you think Haman got what he deserved? Why or why not?

6. Like Queen Esther, we have all been born into this world with great purpose. What can you do to find out about your purpose?

NINETEEN

Zacchaeus

He wanted to see who Jesus was.
LUKE 19:3

I hoisted myself up into the big arms of the sycamore-fig tree. I would wait above the clamor and the crowds for the man of mercy to pass by—the Nazarene. A man called Jesus. He would soon come through the square in Jericho, and I did not want to miss him. I had heard about his miracles and his mercy. I heard Jesus was a friend to all, even to sinners.

I would wait among the branches all day for a glimpse of living grace. Even if it meant to dishonor myself up in a tree. A gust rustled my hair, which had been anointed with perfumed oils just to commemorate this day of the Lord's coming. I settled myself in the curve of the branch, listening to life outside my room of scales, where silver and gold were weighed and collected. A place where people said I knew more of coinage than caring. Perhaps I would die in that place.

The leaves rattled again, making sounds like the chattering children below me. Long ago, I too was like them, talkative and filled with constant wonder, perhaps longing for a noble quest or two. In my youth, I had climbed trees, always wanting to know what it felt like to be the other young men who towered over me. But stunted as I was, growing up, people always liked me, and my father was proud to call me his son.

I am grown and wealthy now, but I have become a man of the earth; I am the dust that men desire to wash from their feet. I am a traitor among my people, a tax commissioner who has been lifted high upon the shoulders of men whose backs are breaking from the burdens of life. I am their burden. My countrymen fear me, hate me for my corruption. The honor I have was imposed; it does not come naturally, as it would for a man who's lived a righteous life.

I am indeed a small man, in stature and in deed. They think of me as prized as the fruit of this sycamore-fig tree—fruit that is only tossed to the swine. Perhaps the Nazarene could redeem my sullied life. Perhaps he could still find in me a remnant of who Zacchaeus was created to be.

In spite of my high perch, I strained to see Jesus. I leaned so far from my limb, I teetered, nearly falling, but I quickly grabbed a branch and steadied myself. I could see him now—Jesus moving through the multitudes. When he reached the spot where I sat in the tree, he looked up. At me! And he called to me, "Zacchaeus, come down immediately. I must stay at your house today."

> *I had heard about his miracles and his mercy.*
> *Jesus was a friend to all, even to sinners.*

Could this be true—that Jesus would not only speak to me, but come to my home? Would he truly enter the house of a publican? This was no ordinary man. I climbed down from my roost at once. I wanted to throw myself down on the ground and kiss the dust near his feet, but I instead bowed with my hand over my heart and replied, "Yes, Rabbi, you are most welcome in my home. Please do come for supper!"

All the people crowded in around us and muttered, "Jesus is going to be the guest of that sinner, Zacchaeus."

I heard their snarling whispers, but instead of despising their chastisements, I embraced them. A public confession poured from my lips, "Look! Here and now I give half of my possessions to the poor, and if I have cheated anybody out of anything, I will pay back four times the amount."

Jesus said, "Today salvation has come to this house, because this man, too, is a son of Abraham. For the Son of Man came to seek and to save the lost."

I heard new murmurings from the crowd, of those who were grateful, and those who doubted my sincerity. But I knew my heart. I knew on this day the captive had been set free from bondage. My soul cried out with the news—yes, deliverance has come to my house!

THE STORY FROM GOD'S WORD
LUKE 19:1-10

Jesus entered Jericho and was passing through. A man was there by the name of Zacchaeus; he was a chief tax collector and was wealthy. He wanted to see who Jesus was, but because he was short he could not see over the crowd. So he ran ahead and climbed a sycamore-fig tree to see him, since Jesus was coming that way.

When Jesus reached the spot, he looked up and said to him, "Zacchaeus, come down immediately. I must stay at your house today." So he came down at once and welcomed him gladly.

All the people saw this and began to mutter, "He has gone to be the guest of a sinner."

But Zacchaeus stood up and said to the Lord, "Look, Lord! Here and now I give half of my possessions to the poor, and if I have cheated anybody out of anything, I will pay back four times the amount."

Jesus said to him, "Today salvation has come to this house, because this man, too, is a son of Abraham. For the Son of Man came to seek and to save the lost."

THE STORY—FROM THEN TO NOW

Each person has a breaking point—when we realize that life is not in our control, and we've come to the end of our human resources to make things right. We can't force life events to go our way, we can't will ourselves to live good lives, and we can't wash ourselves clean from the sins we commit. We are hopeless creatures. When we finally see that truth clearly, we begin our search for someone greater than ourselves to come to our aid.

I think Zacchaeus must have arrived at that crucial spiritual point when he met Jesus. He knew all the gold and silver wasn't going to give him what he wanted in the end, which was to have a pure heart. Finally that longing for redemption outweighed his desire for accumulating wealth. And so when Jesus came through Jericho that day, Zacchaeus was ready to acknowledge Jesus as Lord.

> *Finally that longing for redemption outweighed his desire for accumulating wealth.*

Have you come to that same spiritual crossroads in your life? Redemption is as near to us as Zacchaeus was to Jesus that day. When the Lord looks up into the tree and calls you by name, will you jump down and accept his gift of salvation? When we ask Jesus to forgive us of our sins and acknowledge him as Lord of our lives, we have reason to rejoice as Zacchaeus did! We will be set free from the dark controls of sin, and we will dwell in his glorious house—heaven—for all time.

⊱ THE STORY ⊰
QUESTIONS TO THINK ABOUT

1. Zacchaeus was a wealthy man, in a position that carried some power. Yet he did not seem to mind climbing a tree to get a better view. What might this tell us about Zacchaeus and his desire to see Jesus?

2. Perhaps hoisting himself up that tree revealed just how desperate Zacchaeus was to find redemption. Have you ever felt that kind of spiritual desperation? What did you do about it?

3. My favorite part of the story was when Jesus called Zacchaeus down from the tree and invited himself to stay at the tax collector's house. What part of the story touches your soul? Why?

4. When Zacchaeus made his promises of reform, what do you think the people around him were thinking?

5. Later when Zacchaeus entertained the Lord in his home, what do you think he would have asked Jesus? What might they have talked about?

6. If Jesus said he was coming to your house to stay today, what thoughts would pass through your mind? What would you like to talk with him about?

TWENTY

Elizabeth

When Elizabeth heard Mary's greeting,
the baby leaped in her womb.

LUKE 1:41

I folded the strips of coarse linen cloth that would soon
wrap and swaddle my baby. With lilting fingers I stroked
my womb and the child inside me, growing and blossoming like the rose of Sharon. The infant remained still, unmoving.
He had yet to make his presence known to me, but I had such
peace, knowing God would weave this tiny form into a strong
and hearty child, and he would grow into a devout and godly
man.

This precious son of mine would be given the name of John.
He would be and already was the song of my heart. God had
given me joy. Once I was barren, and now I was with child. He
had removed my disgrace and replaced it with honor. My name,
Elizabeth, means "God's promise," and surely the Almighty
keeps his word!

As I finished folding some clothing and was thinking on all
these things, I heard a knock at my door. On opening it, I saw
my kinswoman Mary. She entered with joyfulness in her countenance and said, "Peace to you, Elizabeth!"

At Mary's greeting, the baby leaped inside me, and a holy
knowing filled my body. *Praise be to God. What a glorious day this*

is! I embraced Mary and welcomed her with a holy kiss. Tears of joy streamed down my face. As if standing in a rain from heaven, I felt drenched in light and joy and laughter. I had never felt so uplifted in spirit, so blessed by God.

I could not suppress my joy for seeing Mary, who was now the mother of my Lord. And even the child within me, my John, surely wanted to cry out amidst these good tidings!

Feeling deeply awed and divinely inspired, I exclaimed, "Blessed are you among women, and blessed is the child you will bear! But why am I so favored, that the mother of my Lord should come to me? As soon as the sound of your greeting reached my ears, the baby in my womb leaped for joy. Blessed is she who has believed that the Lord would fulfill his promises to her!"

THE STORY FROM GOD'S WORD
LUKE 1:39-45

At that time Mary got ready and hurried to a town in the hill country of Judea, where she entered Zechariah's home and greeted Elizabeth. When Elizabeth heard Mary's greeting, the baby leaped in her womb, and Elizabeth was filled with the Holy Spirit. In a loud voice she exclaimed: "Blessed are you among women, and blessed is the child you will bear! But why am I so favored, that the mother of my Lord should come to me? As soon as the sound of your greeting reached my ears, the baby in my womb leaped for joy. Blessed is she who has believed that the Lord would fulfill his promises to her!"

THE STORY—FROM THEN TO NOW

Although God has always met my needs, I've noticed that he rarely follows my schedule. But even if he fails to see the wisdom in my suggestions, God has proven his faithfulness to me just as he proved it to Elizabeth.

One example is my writing life. I've been an author for more than two decades, and during many of those years, my husband and I raised our family. The needs of my kids always came before my career, and that was just the way I wanted it. But many times when I was in the middle of writing a book, I got interrupted. A lot.

I learned that being a mommy meant more than just meeting the basic needs of my kids. It meant more than quality time. It meant quantity time too. So, needless to say, there weren't lavish hours to contemplate the arrangement of words. Even with my commitment to my family, there were days when my humanity showed. I sometimes selfishly wondered when I'd ever be able to focus on my writing. During those times my husband reminded me that when the right time came, God would remember me and he would honor the fact that I'd stayed home with our kids and put the family before my own ambitions.

Even though I couldn't see it at the time, my husband's words were prophetic. When the empty nest came, God did remember me. He did honor my heart's yearning to write—a desire he placed in me even as a young girl. Now I not only have lots of time to write, but my career has blossomed, giving me plenty of satisfying work. Only God can be behind such perfect timing.

> *When the empty nest came, God did remember me.*

Since Elizabeth was beyond child-bearing years, she must have given up hope. But when she heard the news of what God would do, Elizabeth chose to believe God and trust his timetable. He gave her a child who would grow up to be employed in one of the most honorable positions of all time—heralding the coming of Jesus. I think it's safe to say that waiting on God has its benefits. And like Elizabeth, hopefully we'll choose to trust God and his timetable. For blessed are we who believe that the Lord will fulfill his promises!

✦ THE STORY ✦
QUESTIONS TO THINK ABOUT

1. When Elizabeth heard Mary's greeting, the baby leaped inside her womb. What meaning do you think this event was meant to convey?

2. Elizabeth was filled with the Holy Spirit and exclaimed: "Blessed are you among women, and blessed is the child you will bear!" Imagine this dynamic scene and let it continue to play out like a movie. What part of the scene speaks to you most clearly, and why?

3. Why do you think Elizabeth was chosen to be the mother of John the Baptist? What do you think it would have been like to be John's mother?

4. Why do you think Mary came to visit Elizabeth? What support would these two women have to offer each other?

5. God proved his faithfulness to Elizabeth. She rejoiced at the sign of life growing within her. Most humans at one point or another seem to crave a sign from God. Why do you think this is such a universal desire?

6. Think of three examples of God's faithfulness in your life. What does it mean to you to have proof of God's faithfulness?

TWENTY-ONE

Daniel

*There is a man in your kingdom who has the
spirit of the holy gods in him.*

DANIEL 5:11

My soul grieved. Rumors from within the palace—
reports of debaucheries committed by the king and
his guests—reached me. King Belshazzar's heart was
bent on evil day and night. I knew God would not allow his
kingdom to endure. Since his father, Nebuchadnezzar, had died,
there had been no acknowledgment of the one true God.

I strode through the dark corridors and into the main hall,
where the king's banquet was being held. When I approached the
king and his guests, I saw no shame on their faces, even though
what they'd done was detestable in the sight of the Almighty. The
king, including his nobles and concubines, had drunk from the
sacred chalices of gold and silver—the goblets that were to be
used only by the Levitical priests in the temple of God.

A quiet settled over the crowd as they waited for the king to
speak. One of the Babylonian magicians who came to retrieve
me had already explained to me why I was summoned. He told
of a strange vision—fingers of a human hand appearing by the
lampstand and writing on the plaster. No enchanter or astrologer
or diviner could decipher what had been written on the wall.

The writing was large enough for all to see, cryptic enough for all to fear.

The king's face was still white as ash from witnessing the ghostly fingers that moved along the wall. With a trembling voice, he addressed me. "I have heard that the spirit of the gods is in you—that you are able to give interpretations and to solve difficult problems. If you can read this writing and tell me what it means, you will be clothed in purple and have a gold chain placed around your neck, and you will be made the third highest ruler in the kingdom."

I cringed at these last words—I wanted nothing to do with gifts from his hand. After studying the divine words before me, I turned back to King Belshazzar, who was pale and weak, frozen with fear in his royal seat. I could not ease his mind, nor diminish his terror, for he had brought great judgment upon his own head with his blaspheming practices.

Knowing God was with me, I boldly spoke to the king, "You may keep your gifts for yourself and give your rewards to someone else. You have set yourself up against the Lord of heaven. You praised gods, but you did not honor the God who holds in his hand your life and all your ways. Therefore he sent the hand that wrote the inscription: MENE, MENE, TEKEL, PARSIN.

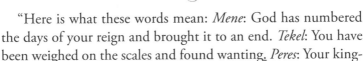

Tekel: *You have been weighed on the scales and found wanting.*

"Here is what these words mean: *Mene*: God has numbered the days of your reign and brought it to an end. *Tekel*: You have been weighed on the scales and found wanting. *Peres*: Your kingdom is divided and given to the Medes and Persians."

Then Belshazzar lowered his head and commanded his officials to clothe me in purple and place a gold chain around my neck. He made the proclamation that I would now be the third highest ruler in the kingdom.

But no decree could save him now. Belshazzar, king of the Babylonians, would be slain this very night.

The Story from God's Word
Daniel 5:17, 22-31

Then Daniel answered the king, "You may keep your gifts for yourself and give your rewards to someone else. Nevertheless, I will read the writing for the king and tell him what it means. . . .

"But you, Belshazzar, his son, have not humbled yourself, though you knew all this. Instead, you have set yourself up against the Lord of heaven. You had the goblets from his temple brought to you, and you and your nobles, your wives and your concubines drank wine from them. You praised the gods of silver and gold, of bronze, iron, wood and stone, which cannot see or hear or understand. But you did not honor the God who holds in his hand your life and all your ways. Therefore he sent the hand that wrote the inscription.

"This is the inscription that was written:
  MENE, MENE, TEKEL, PARSIN
"Here is what these words mean:
  Mene: God has numbered the days of your reign and brought it to an end.
  Tekel: You have been weighed on the scales and found wanting.
  Peres: Your kingdom is divided and given to the Medes and Persians."

Then at Belshazzar's command, Daniel was clothed in purple, a gold chain was placed around his neck, and he was proclaimed the third highest ruler in the kingdom.

That very night Belshazzar, king of the Babylonians, was slain, and Darius the Mede took over the kingdom, at the age of sixty-two.

The Story—from Then to Now

God is full of love—compassionate, but also just. Love requires both attributes, or it's not genuine.

In this story of the writing on the wall, God brought justice to Belshazzar, king of the Babylonians. The king refused to honor God, even though he had learned a powerful lesson from his father about putting pagan gods aside and acknowledging the one true God. Belshazzar was blatant and blasphemous with his defiance, and this rebellious behavior brought on his own destruction.

In contrast we see Daniel, humble and faithful, true to the one Most High God, and willing to speak on his behalf. While Belshazzar was given terror and confusion, Daniel was given insight and intelligence and wisdom.

> *My prayer is that when I'm weighed on the scales of life, I am not found wanting.*

Sometimes it's hard for us to wrap our minds around God's punishment or even his discipline, since it's more comfortable to think of the Almighty as a celestial teddy bear—a being who would never condemn our actions or pronounce judgment. God does indeed dote on his creation with great affection, but he is also mystical, awesome, creative, powerful, resplendent, majestic, beautiful, unfathomable, righteous—and jealous. God is not jealous in human terms. That is, he is not full of resentfulness, suspicion, and prideful retaliation, but God has set certain boundaries, and he will not be mocked. He is the Creator of all things, including us, and he has a right not to sanction the worship of false gods, even if those entities come in the form of money, career, position, family, or . . . well, anything that makes us turn our hearts from him.

My prayer is that when I'm weighed on the scales of life, I am not found wanting like King Belshazzar. I want to be humble, like Daniel, and turn away the prizes of this world to speak the truth that comes from the one God, who holds in his hand our lives and all our ways. At the end of my days, my hope is that I can say I've lived 2 Timothy 4:7—that "I have fought the good fight, I have finished the race, I have kept the faith." And I'm praying the same thing for you.

✎ THE STORY ✎
QUESTIONS TO THINK ABOUT

1. King Belshazzar's heart was bent on evil. Do you think God dealt with the king's sins fairly? Why or why not?

2. We learn in the book of Daniel that ever since the king's father, Nebuchadnezzar, had died, there had been no worship of the one true God. Has our nation's government come to that point, where some of our leaders no longer desire to recognize the one true God?

3. Do you think our nation stands in judgment for this sin?

4. We love to think of God as all love and no justice, or maybe only justice delivered to our enemies. But what would the world look like if that were true, if there were no justice? What would your world look like if you were not disciplined with justice?

5. The most popular secular movies and books portray stories where good triumphs over evil. What do you think are the origins of our desire for good to win?

6. God does not sanction the worship of false gods. Daniel spoke against the king's idolatry. Have you allowed anything to come before God? How can you take a stand against those things in your own life?

7. The prophetic words spoken to the king are haunting: "You have been weighed on the scales and found wanting." We have all been founding wanting. How has God dealt with that truth in your life?

TWENTY-TWO

Rebekah

Before he had finished praying, Rebekah came out with her jar on her shoulder.

GENESIS 24:15

The sun vanished beyond the tents, beyond the dusty town of Nahor. My thoughts always wandered outside my life, outside the boundaries of my home. Hopes formed in my mind like cloud shadows on the desert, like ripples in the well water, always just out of reach. Hopes for marriage to a good man—and for the gift of children.

I adjusted the jug on my shoulder and walked the well-worn path with the other daughters of the town, toward the spring. The cool of evening was upon us, and the young women would soon gather. Already I could hear the chatter of my friends, but my restlessness kept me from listening.

I spotted a caravan approaching, and my heart quickened. Knowing the men who journeyed toward our tents would need water, I hurried to the spring. My skin prickled with a sense of the closeness of the divine. Or was that just the wind? *I feel I will carry more than water home tonight.*

My spirit did not fear. No, my vessel of flesh instead held a twinkling of expectant joy! I went down to the spring, filled my jar, and came up again.

One of the men from the caravan hurried to me and said, "Please give me a little water from your jar."

I noticed the man's knuckles—white in the waning light—as he clutched his staff. He seemed intent on something, even nervous. Perhaps he had come to trade his goods in Nahor and felt pressed to be on his way before dark.

"Drink, my lord," I replied. Then I quickly lowered my jar and gave the man a sip. When he had finished, I said, "I'll draw water for your camels too, until they have had enough to drink."

Not wanting to worry the man with waiting, I emptied my jar with haste into the trough, ran back to the spring to draw more water, and drew enough for all his camels. I could feel the man's eyes on me the entire time.

Why make such an offer? I couldn't explain it—I can't even now. I had never been so bold with other travelers. But I'd felt an urging in my spirit.

> *I could feel the man's eyes on me the entire time.*

The man watched me carefully as I went about my work, but he said nothing. When the camels had finished drinking, the man took out a gold nose ring and two gold bracelets from his pack. Then he asked, "Whose daughter are you? Please tell me, is there room in your father's house for us to spend the night?"

I answered him, "I am Rebekah, the daughter of Bethuel, the son that Milkah bore to Nahor. And we have plenty of straw and fodder, as well as room for you to spend the night."

With a nod of his head, the man handed me the ring and placed the gold bracelets on my arm. Then he bowed down and said, "Praise be to the Lord, the God of my master Abraham, who has not abandoned his kindness and faithfulness to my master. As for me, the Lord has led me on the journey to the house of my master's relatives."

Amazed with the beautiful gifts and the stranger's words, I ran to tell my family all that had happened. I would tell them Abraham's servant brought good news from the land beyond the sun—and I hoped that news would make me a wife and some-day . . . a mother!

THE STORY FROM GOD'S WORD
Genesis 24:15, 19-27

Before he had finished praying, Rebekah came out with her jar on her shoulder. She was the daughter of Bethuel son of Milkah, who was the wife of Abraham's brother Nahor.

After she had given him a drink, she said, "I'll draw water for your camels too, until they have had enough to drink." So she quickly emptied her jar into the trough, ran back to the well to draw more water, and drew enough for all his camels. Without saying a word, the man watched her closely to learn whether or not the Lord had made his journey successful.

When the camels had finished drinking, the man took out a gold nose ring weighing a beka and two gold bracelets weighing ten shekels. Then he asked, "Whose daughter are you? Please tell me, is there room in your father's house for us to spend the night?"

She answered him, "I am the daughter of Bethuel, the son that Milkah bore to Nahor." And she added, "We have plenty of straw and fodder, as well as room for you to spend the night."

Then the man bowed down and worshiped the Lord, saying, "Praise be to the Lord, the God of my master Abraham, who has not abandoned his kindness and faithfulness to my master. As for me, the Lord has led me on the journey to the house of my master's relatives."

THE STORY—FROM THEN TO NOW

Clear and immediate answers to prayer—that is what we long for. Don't we? I know I do. That is exactly what Abraham's servant received when he prayed about Isaac's future wife.

If you want to enjoy the whole miraculous story of how God provided a wife for Isaac, read chapter 24 of Genesis. It relates an

Rebekah ❧ **131**

amazing response from God. In fact, Abraham's servant hadn't even finished his prayer when it was answered! Now, I could deal with that scenario on a daily basis quite well, let me tell you.

Many times God does answer my prayers right away. But not always. Needless to say, I've wondered why. And I've concluded that if we did receive everything we wanted immediately, we would have no need for living a life of faith, which is what we're called to do. And also, I don't truly need everything I ask for. Sometimes over the long haul, I can look back with a grateful heart, thankful that God didn't give me what I'd begged for.

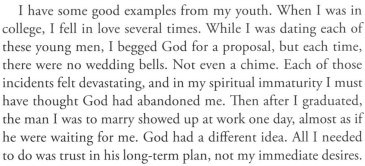

All I needed to do was trust in his long-term plan, not my immediate desires.

I have some good examples from my youth. When I was in college, I fell in love several times. While I was dating each of these young men, I begged God for a proposal, but each time, there were no wedding bells. Not even a chime. Each of those incidents felt devastating, and in my spiritual immaturity I must have thought God had abandoned me. Then after I graduated, the man I was to marry showed up at work one day, almost as if he were waiting for me. God had a different idea. All I needed to do was trust in his long-term plan, not my immediate desires.

So, when our desperate pleas go up to the Almighty, and we wonder when the miracle will ever come, remember how God sometimes works behind the scenes. How he gives us what we need and not merely what we want. And how he may delay the answer to allow us a season of growth. Then when the answer comes, we can do as Abraham's servant did and praise God for his kindness and faithfulness!

1. Abraham's servant hadn't even finished his prayer about his master's future daughter-in-law, when it was answered. How often do you get a clear and immediate answer to your prayers? What prayer are you wanting such an answer for right now?

2. Many times, do your prayers seem to go unanswered? How do you handle those times when prayers seem to pile up? How do you think God wants us to handle those times?

3. If we did receive everything we wanted immediately, would we no longer need to have faith? Why or why not?

4. God cares more about what we need than what we want. Has God ever said no to you, and then later you found out how the "no" was a real blessing in disguise? What happened?

5. Rebekah didn't know that her simple act of giving the man water and watering his camels was the answer to his prayer. She was just fulfilling her daily duty and showing kindness to a stranger. What do you think we can learn from her part in this story?

6. I like the servant's attitude—his guileless heart. What do you like most about this story?

TWENTY-THREE

John the Baptist

John tried to deter him, saying, "I need to be baptized by you, and do you come to me?"
MATTHEW 3:17

First just a few of them came. Then larger groups, then whole villages. The people living in the Judean countryside came to me, to hear the voice of one calling in the wilderness. They came to hear me preach about the Messiah, and to be baptized in the Jordan. As I stood in the warm water, I looked out at their faces and prayed for them to make way in their hearts for the Lord.

There was a stirring in the crowd, and some of the Galileans who had gathered by the shore watched in reverence as a man approached, clearing a path through the people. The man was Jesus of Nazareth.

Jesus stepped into the water and waded toward me from the shallows. His eyes searched me, knew me—we were kinsmen, he and I. His gaze warmed me like the flames of my wilderness campfires. His transforming power and glory radiated around him like a thousand suns.

I said to the crowd, "Look, the Lamb of God, who takes away the sin of the world!"

He had come to be baptized. By me. What could I say to him? I was not even worthy to stoop down and untie his sandals.

Certainly I could not baptize him as if he were a common sinner! "Master, I need to be baptized by you, and do you come to me?"

Jesus replied, "Let it be so now; it is proper for us to do this to fulfill all righteousness."

There were no words to speak, for there was nothing I would deny my Savior. He who knew no sin was willing to be washed. He who deserved our worship, took on the role of a servant. Awe rose in me, and joy rang sweet like the songs of angels. I gave my consent.

Jesus held out his hand, and I clasped his wrist. I pressed my other hand to his back and lowered this man—this Maker of heaven and earth, even of this very river—down into the swirling waters of the Jordan.

As Jesus came up out of the river, water dripped from his clothes, from his beard and his head. But the droplets flashed like swords. The sun burst forth from the clouds and sprayed on us a holy rain, making Jesus resplendent. Then the Spirit of God in the form of a white dove descended from the sky and alighted on Jesus' shoulder.

> *He who knew no sin was willing to be washed.*

A mighty voice rumbled from the heavens, saying, "This is my Son, whom I love; with him I am well pleased."

The crowd gasped, and people shouted, "He is the Messiah!"

I looked up and praised God. Jesus had come into the world—the One who would baptize with the Holy Spirit and with fire!

THE STORY FROM GOD'S WORD
MATTHEW 3:13-17

Then Jesus came from Galilee to the Jordan to be baptized by John. But John tried to deter him, saying, "I need to be baptized by you, and do you come to me?"

Jesus replied, "Let it be so now; it is proper for us to do this to fulfill all righteousness." Then John consented.

As soon as Jesus was baptized, he went up out of the water. At that moment heaven was opened, and he saw the Spirit of God descending like a dove and alighting on him. And a voice from heaven said, "This is my Son, whom I love; with him I am well pleased."

THE STORY—FROM THEN TO NOW

The story of John the Baptist is a remarkable one. Jesus said, "I tell you, among those born of women there is no one greater than John" (Luke 7:28). What a privilege to carry such an inimitable title. But that unique honor came with a heavy price. John lived a life of hardship. He spent time alone, living in the wilderness, not eating the usual Jewish fare, but wild honey and locusts. This kind of life would have taken discipline and devotion.

People listened to John's preaching and repented, but he was also hated by the king for his righteous rebuke. John lost his life in a gruesome manner—all for his faithfulness to his calling, which was to prepare the way for Christ.

When I think of what John sacrificed, including his life, I am deeply humbled. Over the centuries, people have been threatened, tortured, and murdered over the gospel message. What have I done for the kingdom?

I hope at the very least I can be a witness for Christ, a glowing lantern of his resplendent light, speaking the truth of salvation in love. May we strive to be more like John the Baptist, paving the way for Christ, that all may come to know his saving grace. And so that all may praise him, like John, saying, "Look, the Lamb of God, who takes away the sin of the world!" (John 1:29).

❧ THE STORY ❧
QUESTIONS TO THINK ABOUT

1. In my fictional segment, I described Jesus in the way I envision him. How do you think Jesus will look in heaven?

2. Why do you think Jesus wanted to be baptized by John? What was the purpose of this symbolic act?

3. Why was John hesitant in baptizing Jesus? Think about the people who were watching this act. What various kinds of reactions might they have had?

4. John the Baptist lost his life—all for his faithfulness to his calling, which was to prepare the way for Christ. Would you be willing to go that far if necessary—to give up your life for Christ?

5. Baptism is a symbolic and public demonstration of one's faith in Christ. Why do you think water has always been the essential element in this ceremony?

6. What does baptism mean to you?

TWENTY-FOUR

Hannah

*Do not take your servant for a wicked
woman; I have been praying here
out of my great anguish and grief.*

1 SAMUEL 1:16

When I was a girl, I watched my father cut down a
fig tree and cast it into the fire. He had said that
a barren fruit tree was of no worth.

As a woman, in my barren condition, I had come to resemble
that fig tree. Would I too be tossed into the flames for my worth-
lessness? I embraced this thought bitterly, as I had a thousand
times before. But now I came to weep before the house of God.
My skin became damp from the warmth of the sun and the heat
of my sorrow. My anguish spread, finding no borders, knowing
no relief for my loss.

I had been left alone and empty, unsheltered from the cruel-
ties of my rival—my husband's second wife—for she could conceive and was blessed with sons and daughters. Peninnah's womb
had not been closed like a tomb in the wilderness. What had I
done to cause the Lord to look upon me with such disdain?

Over and over, the words of my husband, Elkanah, echoed
inside me. He would say "Hannah, why are you weeping? Why
don't you eat? Why are you downhearted? Don't I mean more to

you than ten sons?" But his kind declarations and gifts, which were meant to comfort, brought me no peace.

One day, when we were finished eating and drinking in Shiloh, I stood up and opened my soul to the Almighty, spilling out my distress before him, begging for his mercy—for favor on his servant. And then I made a vow, saying quietly in my heart, "Lord Almighty, if you will only look on your servant's misery and remember me, and not forget your servant but give her a son, then I will give him to the Lord for all the days of his life. No razor will ever be used on his head."

Even in the midst of my troubled heart and my passionate cry, I could sense that Eli the priest watched me from his chair by the doorpost of the Lord's house. I covered my lips with my trembling fingers, for I realized they had been moving in my private supplication.

Eli pointed his finger at me and said, "How long are you going to stay drunk? Put away your wine."

"Not so, my lord." I wrung my hands, wanting to be understood, desperate not to be wrongly accused. "I am a woman who is deeply troubled. I have not been drinking. I was pouring out my soul to the Lord. Do not take your servant for a wicked woman. I have been praying here out of my great anguish and grief."

Eli answered me, "Go in peace, and may the God of Israel grant you what you have asked of him."

I said to him, "May your servant find favor in your eyes." Then I went home and ate, and my spirit no longer felt downcast.

The Story from God's Word

1 Samuel 1:9-17

Once when they had finished eating and drinking in Shiloh, Hannah stood up. Now Eli the priest was sitting on his chair by the doorpost of the Lord's house. In her deep anguish Hannah prayed to the Lord, weeping bitterly. And she made a vow, saying, "Lord Almighty, if you will only look on your servant's misery and remember me, and not forget your servant but give her a son, then I will give him to the Lord for all the days of his life, and no razor will ever be used on his head."

As she kept on praying to the Lord, Eli observed her mouth. Hannah was praying in her heart, and her lips were moving but her voice was not heard. Eli thought she was drunk and said to her, "How long are you going to stay drunk? Put away your wine."

"Not so, my lord," Hannah replied, "I am a woman who is deeply troubled. I have not been drinking wine or beer; I was pouring out my soul to the Lord. Do not take your servant for a wicked woman; I have been praying here out of my great anguish and grief."

Eli answered, "Go in peace, and may the God of Israel grant you what you have asked of him."

Month after month, year after year, nothing happened.

The Story—from Then to Now

As I read the story of Hannah in the Bible, I was struck with one heart-piercing thought—*this story is about me.* Many years ago I was afflicted with Hannah's malady: I could not conceive. I tried almost everything that the doctor suggested, including fertility drugs and a painful procedure in the hospital that was to help me conceive in the future. Month after month, year after year, nothing happened, except for the sorrow of two miscarriages. Just like Hannah, my grief from not being able to have a child knew no borders.

When I reached a moment of great weariness in my journey, I lowered my head onto the kitchen table and, like Hannah, cried with anguish, begging God to let my husband and me have a child. I thought of all the women who threw away the life inside them through abortion, and wondered about the injustice of it all.

When I rose up from my weeping that day in the kitchen and cleaned my face, I wasn't sure if God would answer my prayer, whether he would give me the desire of my heart. I had faith, but I was scared and tired. Like Hannah, I was remembered; God saw my anguish and gave me life through my husband. We had two beautiful and healthy children, a boy and a girl, and they are the joys of my life. Had I not conceived, we would have adopted, and God would have blessed our decision, I am certain. But I am a witness to the truth that God does hear our cries. He hears and responds in love and wisdom. That we can count on.

⅏ THE STORY ⅏
QUESTIONS TO THINK ABOUT

1. Have you ever suffered like Hannah? How did you deal with your sorrow?

2. Hannah made a vow to God concerning her barrenness. Have you ever made a pledge before the Lord? What happened?

3. Initially, Eli falsely accused Hannah of being drunk, though she was praying. His response must have added to Hannah's grief. What can we learn from Eli's reaction?

4. Throughout the Bible, God shows his compassion on women who long to have children. Do you think their requests for children are especially pleasing to God? Why or why not?

5. To see the happy ending to Hannah's story, read chapters 1 and 2 of 1 Samuel. Not all women who pray for children receive such an answer from God. How can we be sensitive to those who carry this kind of special grief from either experiencing infertility or miscarriage? If you are a person who has experienced this kind of grief, what was a comfort to you?

6. Hannah's character can be glimpsed through the way she responded to her grief, to her husband, to her rival, to Eli, and to her Lord, and in the way those around her responded to her. What wisdom can we glean from reading about Hannah's life? What glimpses of your character would we see if we witnessed your response to others in times of trial and sorrow?

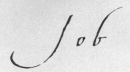

TWENTY-FIVE

You have not spoken the truth
about me, as my servant Job has.

JOB 42:8

I became as useful as the dusky ashes beneath me. I lost all I possessed, and except for my wife, I lost all I love. My children and wealth were swept away by the hand of the Almighty—the One whom I have praised and worshiped all the days of my life. I sewed sackcloth over my skin and buried my brow in the dust. My face was red with weeping; dark shadows ringed my eyes. If my anguish could have been weighed, and all my misery placed on the scales, it would surely have outweighed the sand of the seas.

My friends came to sit with me, to share in my sorrow; but I felt no comfort in their presence. Day and night in silence, I examined my life, searching for reasons that calamity should strike me. But my quest was in vain.

Weary and scarred with boils, I sat and scraped at my sores with a piece of broken pottery. My life was no more than a wilderness, nothing left but dry bones. I shed desperate tears. *Cursed is the day of my birth.*

Finally, I looked toward my friends and gave free rein to my grief. "May the day of my birth perish, and the night that said, 'A boy is conceived!' That day—may it turn to darkness; may God above not care about it; may no light shine on it." I poured out my anguish, and let it flow as a river falls over a precipice. "Why is light given to those in misery, and life to the bitter of soul, to those who long for death that does not come, who search for it more than for hidden treasure?"

> *Their counsel became fierce,*
> *but their compassion failed.*

But instead of offering relief, my friends brought arguments against me. With each speech their outbursts became more and more blustery, like the hot wind that brought the roof down on the heads of my sons and daughters. Their counsel became fierce, but their compassion failed.

Then my friend Eliphaz said, "Would a wise person answer with empty notions or fill their belly with the hot east wind? Would they argue with useless words, with speeches that have no value? But you even undermine piety and hinder devotion to God. Your sin prompts your mouth; you adopt the tongue of the crafty. Your own mouth condemns you, not mine; your own lips testify against you."

When I could take no more of their assaults, I cried out, "How long will you torment me and crush me with words? Ten times you have reproached me; shamelessly you attack me . . ." I turned from their disapproving eyes and raised my face to the heavens. "I know that my redeemer lives, and that in the end he will stand on the earth. And after my skin has been destroyed, yet in my flesh I will see God; I myself will see him with my own eyes—I, and not another. How my heart yearns within me!"

THE STORY FROM GOD'S WORD
JOB 42:7-17

After the Lord had said these things to Job, he said to Eliphaz the Temanite, "I am angry with you and your two friends, because you have not spoken the truth about me, as my servant Job has. So now take seven bulls and seven rams and go to my servant Job and sacrifice a burnt offering for yourselves. My servant Job will pray for you, and I will accept his prayer and not deal with you according to your folly. You have not spoken the truth about me, as my servant Job has." So Eliphaz the Temanite, Bildad the Shuhite and Zophar the Naamathite did what the Lord told them; and the Lord accepted Job's prayer.

After Job had prayed for his friends, the Lord restored his fortunes and gave him twice as much as he had before. All his brothers and sisters and everyone who had known him before came and ate with him in his house. They comforted and consoled him over all the trouble the Lord had brought on him, and each one gave him a piece of silver and a gold ring.

The Lord blessed the latter part of Job's life more than the former part. He had fourteen thousand sheep, six thousand camels, a thousand yoke of oxen and a thousand donkeys. And he also had seven sons and three daughters. The first daughter he named Jemimah, the second Keziah and the third Keren-Happuch. Nowhere in all the land were there found women as beautiful as Job's daughters, and their father granted them an inheritance along with their brothers.

After this, Job lived a hundred and forty years; he saw his children and their children to the fourth generation. And so Job died, an old man and full of years.

The Story—from Then to Now

How many of us, like Job, have cried our faces red from weeping bitter tears at life's sufferings? I certainly have. If you've been alive for any length of time, you'll most likely relate to this book of the Bible more than any other.

If you read the whole book of Job, you'll also find that Job's friends spent more time arguing with him than they did offering him any comfort. Job asked his friends, "How long will you torment me and crush me with words?" (Job 19:2). His so-called friend Eliphaz said Job's lament was full of hot air. He said that Job had condemned himself—that he was not only a sinner but crafty, and his words had no value. Imagine such severe language railed at a man whose pain and loss had been so extreme!

I've known some people over the years who were a great comfort to me when I needed them, and there have been others who seemed clueless when it came to offering compassion. Some people just don't have the right words or attitude. In fact, there are some whose bedside manner is enough to make a die-hard hypochondriac claim instantaneous healing! Instead of coming alongside suffering folks and offering a hand, they bring a bagful of stones to throw. They arrive at the door with mouths full of judgment, which they are happy to spew like a shower of mud. They fancy themselves as offering wise counsel and help, and yet their stinging stones of condemnation leave wounds so deep on our spirits, it takes months to recover.

> *Some people just don't have*
> *the right words or attitude.*

In the book of Job, God made it clear that he was not pleased with Job's friends. In the end, God does challenge Job, but his righteous anger is pointed at Job's friends for not speaking the truth about him. In fact, he commands Job's friends to repent and to ask Job to pray for them. Talk about being humbled by the Almighty!

In light of the message from the book of Job, perhaps one of the best prayers is, "Lord, may the bag I carry always be filled with cake to share with my friends and not stones to throw at them!"

❧ THE STORY ❧
QUESTIONS TO THINK ABOUT

1. I doubt that any of us has suffered as Job did, but every person has her own darkest moments, when hope is dimmed, if not extinguished for a time. What has helped you through your darkest moments?

2. To understand the messages of the life of Job better, read the entire book of Job. It's full of insight into the nature of our Creator. In the first chapter, we see God seeming to make a deal with Satan. What are we to make of this part of the story?

3. When God allowed Satan to attack Job, what did you think? Did you think of it as an unfair test? What do you think this story teaches us about adversity?

4. When you've been in the middle of hard times, have you ever had friends who've added to your grief by finding fault with you instead of comforting you? How have you responded?

5. How do you think Job's experience with his friends changed their relationship? What lessons do you think Job took away from his conversations with his so-called friends during this troubled time?

6. Job's friends were worthless at comforting him in his great hour of suffering. They did what many people do in times of suffering—they fill the awkward silences with empty words. Sometimes those words actually do harm. But is there anything of value that can be found in the words of Job's friends? If so, what is it?

TWENTY-SIX

Miriam

All the women followed her,
with timbrels and dancing.

EXODUS 15:20

W ater can give life, and water can steal life away. I learned both these truths as a young girl, watching my mother cry as she set my baby brother floating on the Nile—the river which brought him safely to the arms of a princess and back again to his mother's breast.

I listened now as that same brother sang praise to God: "Who among the gods is like you, Lord?" The churning sea that had been divided by a powerful east wind and held back by the mighty hand of God had been released. Liberated from its confining walls, the water crashed down with such thundering force, it took our breath away. I stood at a distance, looking out over the Red Sea, amazed by the majesty of the God who worked these wonders.

Pharaoh, who had been pursuing us with his men, had been swept away in the violent waters, along with his horses, chariots, and horsemen. Then the foaming surge crashed and covered over them all, silencing their screams.

Children clung to me, frightened at the sight, but I soothed them. "The Egyptians will harm us no more." We would no longer know captivity; we would no longer be crushed in the relentless oppression of slavery. Though weary and dusty, we were free. Our liberty stood before us, like a flowing river to the sea.

"Miriam, such a miracle, isn't it?" My brother Aaron stood at the edge of the sea and smiled. "God has slain our enemies. We have been saved by his mighty hand."

"This great wonder of God," I said to my brother, "will be spoken of and written about until time ends."

A mist came up from the sea and the cooling spray revived us. Shouts of praise rose up from my fellow Israelites. Tears of gladness ran down my face as words of adoration filled my spirit. I could no longer hold back. I remembered how Aaron had frowned at me when I had refused to leave behind my favorite instrument of worship—he thought we should take only what was needed. But I had told him, "I will need to praise my God again." I took my timbrel from my satchel, raised my hands, and shook it.

> *Though weary and dusty, we were free.*

The other women retrieved their timbrels, and flutes and harps and lyres, from their packs. All of us formed rows and together we swayed—and then danced and sang before God, thanking him for our victory. "Sing to the Lord, for he is highly exalted. Both horse and driver he has hurled into the sea!"

THE STORY FROM GOD'S WORD
EXODUS 15:19-21

When Pharaoh's horses, chariots and horsemen went into the sea, the Lord brought the waters of the sea back over them, but the Israelites walked through the sea on dry ground. Then Miriam the prophet, Aaron's sister, took a timbrel in her hand, and all the women followed her, with timbrels and dancing. Miriam sang to them:

Sing to the Lord,
for he is highly exalted.

Both horse and driver
he has hurled into the sea.

THE STORY—FROM THEN TO NOW

The parting of the Red Sea is certainly one of the most memorable and spectacular miracles in the Bible. But for the Hebrews it was only one of many supernatural deliverances they experienced during their exodus from Egypt and their years in the desert.

One would naturally think the Israelites would never lack for faith, being constantly wowed with so many miracles and being in fellowship with the Almighty through Moses. But trust in their heavenly Father failed so many times, and their demands and grumbling and idolatry got so blatant, that it brought the wrath of God down on their heads. The signs and wonders were no longer enough to sustain their faith in the Almighty. They floundered. Even the ones we might expect to have known better, such as Miriam, who had intimate knowledge of Moses' special relationship with God—even she would one day forget this day of praise and dance and eventually stumble in her faith.

Though the miracles I've seen from the hand of God haven't been as dramatic as the parting of the Red Sea, they have been grand and powerful and welcome when they arrived. In fact, some years ago I created a journal where I recorded God's answers to my prayers—I called it "The Little Book of Miracles." Every time I go back and read about those divine interventions, I'm always amazed.

What is it about humans and their longing for signs and wonders? We crave them, almost to the point of addictions. God answers our prayers, and we beg for more. When we don't get immediate answers, we start to doubt and grumble like the Israelites.

But when he answers, do we even stop to praise him? How often do we have our voices—our instruments of worship—ready to praise the God who is like no other god? Perhaps we need to write down our miracles from God not only on paper but on our hearts, so that when seasons of trials come—when we feel rocked to our core with tragedy—we are armed and ready with a faith that is unshakable and praise that we cannot hold back.

◆ THE STORY ◆
QUESTIONS TO THINK ABOUT

1. God helped the Israelites, but they still had to exercise some faith as they walked through the parted Red Sea and saw those two walls of churning waters. They had to know God well enough to know he hadn't rescued them just to let them drown. Even today, God doesn't always lead us around the sea, but sometimes he takes us right through the middle of it. Even though he's watching over us, we still must believe that ultimately, God has us safe in his keeping. Have you experienced that kind of faith? What happened?

2. After God led the Israelites through the Red Sea on dry ground and then destroyed their enemies, Miriam the prophet broke out into song. Imagine that scene. What words would you use to describe their emotions?

3. Miriam is one of those characters in the Bible who is mentioned very little, but must have had quite a powerful influence on those around her. As sister of the leader of the Israelites, it's easy to imagine she would have been a leader among the women of that community. And she was a key player in the saving of baby Moses. Why do you think it was important for her to lead the women in praise?

4. We may not be prophets, and we may not be sisters of the leaders of nations, but we as women of faith can have great influence on the other women in our communities. Do you acknowledge that you have this role? How have you been influenced by other women in your church?

5. The Hebrews witnessed many supernatural events during their exodus from Egypt and their years in the desert. Why do you think they required more and more assurances and miracles from God? What brought about their lack of faith?

6. What can this story teach us about faith in our modern world?

7. It's easy to forget all the little and big ways that God intervenes in our lives, so a journal to record prayers and miracles can be helpful. It really can become a tool for worship. What is your favorite instrument of praise? What helps you remember to praise and thank God for all he has done for you?

TWENTY-SEVEN

Tabitha

Turning toward the dead woman, he said,
"Tabitha, get up." She opened her eyes,
and seeing Peter she sat up.

ACTS 9:40

"Tabitha, get up." My body shuddered at the command. My head turned to the side, and my eyes opened to the dim light that streamed in through the window.

A man knelt near me.

He watched me with such a potent stare, I could not take my gaze from him. "I was very ill, was I not?" I asked him in a stuttering manner. My throat was as dry as flour fresh from the millstone.

"Yes," the man replied, speaking more softly to me now, "with a fever."

I touched my parched lips with my hands, which had been wrapped in linen. I strained to be free of the wrappings. Then I remembered and stopped my struggle. "Women . . . many of them . . . were crying for me. My dear friends. And then I was no more. I was not among the living. But still . . . I knew myself. I could hear the weeping, see them, even though I was no longer locked within my flesh." I looked at the man again. "You are Peter."

"I am." Peter nodded as he stroked his beard. "But it is Jesus, our Lord, who has brought you back to life."

"I shall praise our Lord every day that he chooses to give me." Sea air drifted in through the window of my upper room, reviving my spirit. I took in a deep, rich breath and sat up.

"I praise the Lord with you." Peter stood from his kneeling. "There has been weeping all over Joppa because of your death. You were remembered well for your good deeds, your sewing of warm garments for those who needed them. But I fear there will be a fresh wave of crying when they see you." His eyes held a twinkle I had remembered from our first meeting. "But this time, only tears of joy." Peter reached out his hand to me.

"Good," I said to him. "I am well now, and there is much work to do."

Peter smiled and helped me up.

> *"I am well now, and there is much work to do."*

THE STORY FROM GOD'S WORD
ACTS 9:36-41

In Joppa there was a disciple named Tabitha (in Greek her name is Dorcas); she was always doing good and helping the poor. About that time she became sick and died, and her body was washed and placed in an upstairs room. Lydda was near Joppa; so when the disciples heard that Peter was in Lydda, they sent two men to him and urged him, "Please come at once!"

Peter went with them, and when he arrived he was taken upstairs to the room. All the widows stood around him, crying and showing him the robes and other clothing that Dorcas had made while she was still with them.

Peter sent them all out of the room; then he got down on his knees and prayed. Turning toward the dead woman, he said, "Tabitha, get up." She opened her eyes, and seeing Peter she sat up. He took her by

the hand and helped her to her feet. Then he called for the believers,
especially the widows, and presented her to them alive.

The Story—from Then to Now

Have you ever known a Tabitha kind of person? That is, a person who shows thanks to Christ for his sacrifice and salvation by giving to others in his name? For me, growing up, Tabitha showed up in the form of my father, Edwin Breitling. He was a wheat farmer in western Oklahoma, and raised cattle and hogs commercially as well. My father also had a huge orchard and garden to feed his family. Come harvest time there was always more produce than we could ever eat, so instead of letting the fruits and vegetables rot on the branch or vine, he boxed them up and drove them into town to give to people who were in need.

My father never once preached at me, telling me how I needed to remember to give to the needy. Instead he offered me far more valuable lessons—in his actions.

Over the years I've had the joy of observing many Tabithas come and go through my life, women who desired to live quiet but memorable lives, women who changed the world—one cup of cool water at a time. All because they had the heart of a servant and a love for Christ.

Who's the Tabitha in your realm of influence?

☞ THE STORY ☜
Questions to Think About

1. Try to imagine the scene when Peter presented the newly risen Tabitha to her friends. How do you think they reacted?

2. Tabitha's friends grieved deeply for her. She had been a great woman, always doing good and helping the poor. She was beloved, and people truly mourned her absence. What a powerful statement about her life! Have you ever wondered what people will say at your funeral someday? What things would you like them to say? What do you want to be remembered for?

3. This story shows us one example of many in the New Testament of physical healing through the power of Christ. But there is still a limited number of these examples. In other words, not everyone who came in contact with Jesus or his apostles was healed in a physical sense. What can we learn from this fact?

4. Sometimes self-sacrifice takes a backseat to self-satisfaction. Our world urges us to go after the latter, but God rewards the former. If you are honest, which worldview most often motivates you in the morning? Why?

5. My father was the Tabitha influence in my life. Think of a few Tabithas in your life and what makes them like this great woman from the Bible. Perhaps one of the Tabithas in your life is you!

TWENTY-EIGHT

Mary Magdalene

Early on the first day of the week, while it was still dark, Mary Magdalene went to the tomb.

JOHN 20:1

I stood outside the tomb, crying tears of anguish. As I wept, I bent over to look into the sepulcher where my Savior had been placed. Two figures, brilliant as the sun, sat where Jesus' body had been placed—one sat at the head and the other at the foot. These heavenly beings glowed with sublime splendor. Such light and goodness emanated from them, I shielded my eyes from their radiance. The two figures were nothing like the foul spirits from my past—the seven demons that had tormented my body and spirit every waking step, every dreaming hour.

The two angels asked me, "Woman, why are you crying?"

"They have taken my Lord away," I said to them, "and I don't know where they have put him." Searching with my eyes for a sign, I turned around and saw a gardener standing not far from a row of lilies.

The caretaker asked me, "Woman, why are you crying? Who is it you are looking for?"

"Sir, if you have carried him away, tell me where you have

put him, and I will get him." I rubbed my eyes and peered at the man, trying to make out his face in the glow coming from the tomb.

The man's tone softened. "Mary."

Right away I recognized him and cried out in Aramaic, "Rabboni!" I rushed to him and embraced him, not wanting to let go of him.

Jesus said, "Do not hold on to me, for I have not yet ascended to the Father. Go instead to my brothers and tell them, 'I am ascending to my Father and your Father, to my God and your God.'"

"Yes, Lord, I will tell them all." I took in his presence once more, reluctant to leave him. But in obedience I turned away and hurried from there, stumbling on stones and roots, and nearly falling, but not caring about my steps. I snatched up a branch and whipped it, waving it in the air like a child. I felt light and free, as I had that day of my deliverance, when my torment was no more. *Jesus is alive!* The demons have no victory, death no sting. My heart is full of music—praise is on my lips!

"I have seen the Lord!"

The Story from God's Word

John 20:11-18

Now Mary stood outside the tomb crying. As she wept, she bent over to look into the tomb and saw two angels in white, seated where Jesus' body had been, one at the head and the other at the foot.

They asked her, "Woman, why are you crying?"

"They have taken my Lord away," she said, "and I don't know where they have put him." At this, she turned around and saw Jesus standing there, but she did not realize that it was Jesus.

He asked her, "Woman, why are you crying? Who is it you are looking for?"

Thinking he was the gardener, she said, "Sir, if you have carried him away, tell me where you have put him, and I will get him."

Jesus said to her, "Mary."

She turned toward him and cried out in Aramaic, "Rabboni!" (which means "Teacher").

Jesus said, "Do not hold on to me, for I have not yet ascended to the Father. Go instead to my brothers and tell them, 'I am ascending to my Father and your Father, to my God and your God.'"

Mary Magdalene went to the disciples with the news: "I have seen the Lord!" And she told them that he had said these things to her.

> *The light of Christ must surely appear more brilliant when one is consumed in darkness.*

THE STORY—FROM THEN TO NOW

Recently when I read this passage of Scripture surrounding Mary Magdalene and the risen Christ, I got tearful. Reading their exchange was like looking through an ancient window, catching a glimpse of the awe-inspiring but compassionate character of our Lord. Mary Magdalene loved her Savior dearly, for he had not only forgiven her, but he'd delivered her from seven demons.

The light of Christ must surely appear more brilliant when one is consumed in darkness. Mary had wrestled with demon possession, and those spirits must have been a daily torture. She chose to enter into the light of Christ and was eternally grateful for it.

But even though most of us do not live with the drama and torment of demon possession, we are all sinners. We are all fallen creatures, and we are in need of a Savior in the worst way. We have run so far from his divine goodness, that sometimes we don't even recognize our desperate need, our poverty of spirit. We instead whitewash our lives, trying to make ourselves look good enough for heaven, but our finest intentions and our most selfless acts let us reach only a shade of gray, at best.

To achieve a pure white, we have to soak in all the light—something we'll never accomplish on our own. But through

Jesus' blood shed for us, through him taking on our darkness, we can be made white as snow. All we need to do is know that he is God, ask for forgiveness for our offenses, and walk away from our worldly shadows and into the one true Light of the world.

It's no wonder then that Mary wanted to hold on to her Lord, to bask in his glory. After knowing such a fearsome journey and suffering through the grief of mourning, the sight of her Lord's face in that morning light must have been a most welcome one to her heart. It was a sight that brought her profound joy and peace.

In this life, all of us have been on a fearsome journey of one kind or another, and I pray we all keep seeking the light of Jesus' face—to bask in his glory, to shed our suffering, and to receive his profound joy and peace.

THE STORY
Questions to Think About

1. Christ is the light of the world, and this story reflects that truth beautifully. But why do you think the world—when it's so desperately in need of the light—flees from it so often?

2. Imagine the scene when Mary first recognizes Jesus' voice. What is meaningful about this scene to you?

3. We aren't given much information about Mary Magdalene's life, but in my mind she has come to symbolize all humanity and our great need for a Savior. She shows us what it's like to be so grateful for the gift of new life—for grace—that she follows Jesus no matter where he leads. How do you express your gratitude for the gift of grace?

4. How would you describe your relationship with Jesus? Do you feel close to him, like a friend? Or is his voice unfamiliar? What do you want your relationship with Jesus to be like?

5. Jesus said to Mary, "Do not hold on to me, for I have not yet ascended to the Father. Go instead to my brothers and tell them, 'I am ascending to my Father and your Father, to my God and your God.'" Why do you think Jesus said these things to Mary? Why would he trust her with his message?

6. What kind of urgency do you feel in getting Christ's message out to the world? How important to you is it to tell others about Jesus' sacrifice and gift of grace?

TWENTY-NINE

Elijah

The word of the Lord came to Elijah.
1 KINGS 17:2

I am like the wind of the desert—the way it drifts and quickens and dies away at the command of the Almighty. The wind moans through the junipers, lonely and friendless, for who can embrace the wind? I am merely a messenger with news that few heed and no one welcomes.

Daybreak arrived in the Kerith Ravine, east of the Jordan, and as instructed by the Lord, I hid myself in this quiet place. God had promised to care for me. I was hungry and weary, but I had not lost my devotion. God is faithful; he would sustain me during the ravaging drought—a dearth that had struck the land because of the sin of King Ahab.

I heard the cry of a bird and looked upward. The promise of God unfolded before me. A lone raven shadowed the firmament. The winged creature was soon joined by others. They dove and circled as one, their flock of hundreds transforming into a sphere of black. The fearsome sight divided again as they landed on the ground not far from me, their indigo wings shimmering.

Their dark eyes assessed me, as if knowing why they had come. At once the beasts dropped what was held tightly in their beaks, but they made no move to gobble up their feast. They instead hopped backward and made rustling sounds, their wings fluttering swiftly and softly.

Ravens were common beasts of the air. A raven was the first animal to be released by Noah for the purpose of seeking land after the great flood. They were scavengers. And now they were messengers of God—as I was. My heart softened toward the creatures, and I stepped toward the flock. At once, they lifted off as one and disappeared into the morning sky.

> *If God sent a prophet like Elijah today,*
> *I doubt anyone would welcome him,*
> *let alone heed his warnings.*

I gathered the bits of meat and bread offerings from the birds, drank from the brook, and then rested under a willow. I fell into a deep slumber, knowing God had remembered me—he had saved me.

Time passed, and the ravens still obeyed the Lord's instructions, bringing my food morning and evening, but one morning I found the stream where I'd quenched my thirst had dried up. I walked through the ravine, searching for a spring or pool, any sign of water. I found none. No leaves stirred in the breeze, for they had blown away. The sky ached for a single cloud, for a promise of rain. Dust whipped through the circling air, stinging my flesh.

Where could I go? I was like the wind. I sat on the dry stones in the streambed and waited upon the Lord. For even when streams vanished, when life failed, he would be my deliverer.

THE STORY FROM GOD'S WORD

1 KINGS 17:2-7

Then the word of the Lord came to Elijah: "Leave here, turn eastward and hide in the Kerith Ravine, east of the Jordan. You will drink from the brook, and I have directed the ravens to supply you with food there."

So he did what the Lord had told him. He went to the Kerith Ravine, east of the Jordan, and stayed there. The ravens brought him bread and meat in the morning and bread and meat in the evening, and he drank from the brook.

Some time later the brook dried up because there had been no rain in the land.

THE STORY—FROM THEN TO NOW

Elijah was a divine messenger. God used him to warn people when they had strayed into sin. Being a prophet can't be a popular job, since it often means rebuking people. Reprimands are painful and embarrassing—who would seek out the company of a person from whose mouth such words would be bound to come?

We all like to think we are wise and good, but sometimes we aren't. Over the years I've seen people plummeting toward destruction in a host of immoral ways, and yet I remained silent. Why? Because I wanted to be liked. I didn't want anyone to be uncomfortable. I chose the way of amiability. I wanted to sit on the fence and smile. We can choose to put a car in neutral, but we don't have this option in the Christian life.

We aren't always called to be agreeable, but we are commanded to have love in our hearts and truth on our tongues. That doesn't give us carte blanche to blast people verbally whenever we disagree with them. It's tempting, but not good. However, if we see a tide of blatant sin and pretend no one's getting washed under, then we are not following Christ's example.

If God sent a prophet like Elijah today, I doubt anyone would welcome him, let alone heed his warnings. People would laugh before they would listen. In fact, the media would decimate him. Having light sprayed on our individual sins or the transgressions of an entire nation makes us want to squirm or run away or shake our fists. Anything but repent, which is what we are called to do when we have strayed from the One who created us, the One who knows us best—and still loves us best.

But we can learn a new way—to speak the truth in love about sin, including our own. To explore the Bible so we'll know what the truth really is. And to pray for our world, that we might all yearn to lean on God's sustenance more than on people's support.

⊱ THE STORY ⊰
QUESTIONS TO THINK ABOUT

1. Elijah must have lived a lonely kind of existence. When you're a prophet with bad news, not many people want to listen. Has anyone ever given you advice or guidance about your walk with the Lord that was true, but not so easy to hear? How did you respond?

2. The Lord told Elijah, "You will drink from the brook, and I have directed the ravens to supply you with food there." God followed through with his promise, and just about the time Elijah might have gotten comfortable with the arrangement, the brook dried up where he had been living. How do you think this situation might have tested Elijah's faith?

3. Read the rest of I Kings 17. What do you learn there about Elijah's faith?

4. Elijah was in the business of correcting people who had sinned. Why do you think God used prophets, rather than some other means of getting the word out?

5. How effective do you think prophets would be today in our society? Why?

6. What are some ways we can speak the truth with a loving attitude?

THIRTY

Lydia

She was a worshiper of God.
ACTS 16:14

My life is colored purple—a symbol of royalty. Purple has brought prosperity to my house and given splendor to my garments. Even the stains on my fingers come from the precious and costly dye I trade and sell.

But with all my household's wealth and influence, my spirit longed for more. There was a restlessness I could not explain or even fathom. Just as the river curled around the bend, so was my life to turn. These impressions came to me as I sat by the river that runs just beyond the city of Thyatira, where I gather each Sabbath with other women to pray and worship Yahweh.

As we finished our prayers, several men approached us, coming from the direction of the city gate. I did not recognize them. Their steps seemed weary, but their expressions friendly, full of expectation.

"Greetings," one of the men said, whose name I later learned was Paul. He introduced his companions to all of us there by the riverbank and began to tell about a man named Jesus.

I had heard of this man, but I wanted to know more. My relatives who were with me and the other women gathered around, for their interest was piqued as well.

Paul said, "I am a missionary of Christ Jesus, the Messiah, the son of the living God."

My heart stirred. I listened to Paul's every word about Jesus. I could see that the man had a message I needed to hear, that I was destined to hear.

Paul looked at each of us to catch our attention and then said, "Jesus was born of a virgin through the power of the Holy Spirit. He was without sin, and innocent of any crimes, and yet he willingly gave up his life for us. Jesus was crucified and buried, and on the third day he rose from the dead and showed himself to many before his ascension into heaven. Through his sacrifice on the cross, he carried the burden of our sins on his shoulders. And with his resurrection he has broken the bonds of death."

> *"I have waited for this holy one,*
> *this Jesus, all my life."*

The women murmured with excitement among themselves.

"Praise be to God," I said, but wanted to shout. Paul was speaking the words that had already been written on my heart.

Paul waited for us to quiet our chatter and then said, "Jesus, the Messiah, is the answer to this emptiness you feel." He placed his fist over where his heart beat inside his chest. "Jesus came to release you from your bondage of sin. And to give you a home in heaven."

How could this man, Paul—this stranger—know of my emptiness, that gnawing restlessness? Surely he was a messenger from God. I stood up from the rock where I'd been seated. "Teacher, what must I do?"

Paul held out his arms. "Believe in him, and you will be saved."

"I do believe." I gazed at the stains on my hands. "I have waited for this holy one, this Jesus, all my life."

Paul dipped his fingers into the water and said, "Would you be baptized?"

I removed my purple veil and let it drift down to the rocks. "Right here, where I first heard and believed."

THE STORY FROM GOD'S WORD
ACTS 16:11-15

From Troas we put out to sea and sailed straight for Samothrace, and the next day we went on to Neapolis. From there we traveled to Philippi, a Roman colony and the leading city of that district of Macedonia. And we stayed there several days.

On the Sabbath we went outside the city gate to the river, where we expected to find a place of prayer. We sat down and began to speak to the women who had gathered there. One of those listening was a woman from the city of Thyatira named Lydia, a dealer in purple cloth. She was a worshiper of God. The Lord opened her heart to respond to Paul's message. When she and the members of her household were baptized, she invited us to her home. "If you consider me a believer in the Lord," she said, "come and stay at my house." And she persuaded us.

THE STORY—FROM THEN TO NOW

After Lydia's conversion by the river she had a heart to serve God and to care for his missionaries whenever there was a need. Even when they were fresh out of prison.

I love that. I have a willingness to serve God too, but I usually like to call the shots. In other words, I feel so much better about giving of my time if I'm in control of the situation and ask a few questions first. Such as, "What kind of work is it?" and "How much time is it going to take?" I also wonder about things like, "Will this work make me uncomfortable?" or "Will I have to work alongside folks I don't know or don't like?"

Be honest now—have you ever had those thoughts when you were asked to volunteer at church? or anywhere? Perhaps we are a little too human at times. I know I am.

The question is, how can I be more like Lydia? I thought of seven ways that might be helpful.

1. Remember what we are without Christ. Lost. Remember

the peace and redemption he brought us. Giving back is like sending Jesus a thank-you card.

2. Every time I step out in faith to do what God has called me to do, I please him.

3. Those who love God should arise in the morning as Jesus did—as a servant.

4. As believers in Christ, we are the light. We are to show the world how this living and loving thing is really done. And giving of ourselves is a vital part of advancing the kingdom of God.

6. We can't say yes to all who come to us for help, but we can keep our hearts open to God's voice—telling us when to say no and when to say yes—even if the task looks menial, uncomfortable, difficult, time-consuming, or squirmy.

7. Know that if we set out on a mission for God, he will give us the strength and the abilities and the patience to get the job done.

Are we ready to be used by God—with no strings attached?

❧ THE STORY ❧
QUESTIONS TO THINK ABOUT

1. After Lydia's conversion, she used her home to help the cause of Christ. What do you think—has the gift of hospitality changed since biblical times? How so?

2. What other characters in the Bible had the heart to serve like Lydia?

3. Why do you think some people succumb to the mind-set that if they aren't wealthy like Lydia, or if they don't have a model home, they can't open their homes to others? Has anything ever kept you from offering help to those who needed it? If so, what was it?

4. We help the Lord, not in an effort to gain acceptance into heaven, but to thank him for the gift of salvation. What are the many ways we can use our time, talents, and possessions for the kingdom of God?

5. Lydia was already a worshiper of God, before Paul began to speak. But then the "Lord opened her heart." Have you ever worshiped God with your words, but not with your heart? What happened to change that in you? Or, if you are in that position now, what needs to change?

THIRTY-ONE

The Queen of Sheba

*When the queen of Sheba heard about
the fame of Solomon and his relationship
to the Lord, she came to test Solomon
with hard questions.*

1 KINGS 10:1

hat is wisdom, but to live in the light of heaven—to know the mind of God? I heard of a ruler who'd been given a view of the divine, a man who could see the mysteries of life—unravel the mystic perplexities of humankind. He could speak with knowledge concerning the land and sea and heavens. This man, this great king, was Solomon.

I journeyed far to come into his presence, to witness and examine these wonders with the hope that a portion of his knowledge might fall upon me, and so that I might return to my land with resources never known by my people. To lead them with an insightful hand and to share with them what I could learn of the God said to be above all gods—the mighty One whom Solomon and his people worshiped. I had many questions on my mind.

Dressed in my finest regalia and my most splendid crown

and jewels, I came into Solomon's courts and stepped up to his throne. The king was not only handsome in stature but commanding in his demeanor.

I studied him for a moment and then began asking him the questions I had come to challenge him with. He answered every one; nothing was too hard for the king.

At last I said, "The report I heard in my own country about your achievements and your wisdom is true. But I did not believe these things until I saw them with my own eyes. Indeed, not even half was told me; in wisdom and wealth you have far exceeded the report I heard. How happy your people must be! How happy your officials, who continually stand before you and hear your wisdom! Praise be to the Lord your God, who has delighted in you and placed you on the throne of Israel."

King Solomon stepped down from his throne and approached me. "Your words of tribute honor me, and my gratitude is overflowing, but my nobility and distinction are God's gift. Without his wisdom I am left in shadow, with nothing to light my way but folly . . . a chasing after the wind."

I answered the king, "Your humility equals your wisdom, and together they make you more luminous than any man in my kingdom, any star in the heavens." I bowed to him. "I have brought a great caravan of gifts. Please accept my offerings of spices, gold, and precious stones."

Solomon raised his scepter. "I am grateful and indebted to you for your generosity."

> *He answered every one; nothing was too hard for the king.*

Then the sun shone down through the columns from the opening in the roof, making the opulent room and the gilded lions on the steps glisten and flash like fire. "The stories of your wisdom will be passed down through all the generations. My kingdom will recede, but you, my Lord, will be remembered for all time for your greatness."

But once the words had flowed from my lips, a cloud overshadowed the sun and snatched away the glistening splendor from the room. So much so, the day appeared for a moment as twilight. Perhaps it was a sign from God—a warning. Without God's glory, without his approving hand over man's dominions, life would indeed be in shadow and there would be nothing left but folly. A chasing after the wind.

THE STORY FROM GOD'S WORD
1 KINGS 10:1-9

When the queen of Sheba heard about the fame of Solomon and his relationship to the Lord, she came to test Solomon with hard questions. Arriving at Jerusalem with a very great caravan—with camels carrying spices, large quantities of gold, and precious stones— she came to Solomon and talked with him about all that she had on her mind. Solomon answered all her questions; nothing was too hard for the king to explain to her. When the queen of Sheba saw all the wisdom of Solomon and the palace he had built, the food on his table, the seating of his officials, the attending servants in their robes, his cupbearers, and the burnt offerings he made at the temple of the Lord, she was overwhelmed.

She said to the king, "The report I heard in my own country about your achievements and your wisdom is true. But I did not believe these things until I came and saw with my own eyes. Indeed, not even half was told me; in wisdom and wealth you have far exceeded the report I heard. How happy your people must be! How happy your officials, who continually stand before you and hear your wisdom! Praise be to the Lord your God, who has delighted in you and placed you on the throne of Israel. Because of the Lord's eternal love for Israel, he has made you king to maintain justice and righteousness."

THE STORY—FROM THEN TO NOW

Solomon had a glorious beginning in his reign as king of Israel. God came to Solomon in a dream and granted him whatever he wanted. Solomon asked for wisdom, and God was so pleased with the king's choice that he gave him not only wisdom, but honor and wealth as well. Solomon was devoted to God and built a magnificent temple in his name. The king became renowned, which was the reason the queen of Sheba traveled to meet him.

> *Sin has a way of thriving within the fertile soil of our own agendas.*

The king's fame was an important development, since the Israelites were meant to be a showcase people. They were a special chosen people, set apart to tell the world about the one true God.

As the queen of Sheba pointed out, God had placed Solomon on the throne. Sin, however, got the upper hand during this man's reign. One of the ways he disobeyed God was by marrying foreign women. These wives encouraged him to worship other gods, and he did. God found this act of worshiping pagan idols detestable, so he punished Solomon and divided his kingdom after his death. Solomon's beginning was impressive, but his ending was riddled with spectacular disobedience.

Solomon's defiance may have started slowly and innocuously, but he became more and more determined to follow his own path. He surrounded himself with people who, instead of asking him the hard questions, just went along with his choices and encouraged him.

Sin is just as wily today as it was back in the Old Testament. How many times have I been guilty of doing that very thing—speeding right ahead and doing what I know is wrong? And all the while, I'm carrying around my tidy little list of reasons why it's a good idea, in spite of God's warnings. Sin has a way of thriving within the fertile soil of our own agendas. So subtle yet insidious is sin, when left unmonitored it can seriously damage or destroy our relationship with God.

If the wisest man on earth can fall into such profound spiritual decay, what chance does the rest of the world have?

There is real hope. A good solid place to start is to surround yourself with voices who will challenge you—to make a regular habit of prayer, which means listening to God, as well as talking to him. Reading God's living Word and worshiping and fellowshiping at a Bible-believing church is vital for staying the course. And making yourself accountable to godly friends can also be helpful in fleeing from temptation.

To live a perfect life on this side of eternity is not possible in our flesh, but we can—like Solomon's father, David—live not as if chasing after the wind, but as if chasing after God's own heart.

❧ THE STORY ❧
QUESTIONS TO THINK ABOUT

1. When the queen of Sheba heard about the fame of Solomon and his relationship to the Lord, she came to test Solomon with hard questions. What does this tell you about her as a leader?

2. If you had the same opportunity, what questions would you have for King Solomon?

3. When the queen of Sheba saw all the wisdom of Solomon and all his wealth and honor, she was overwhelmed. Have you ever been in a place that overwhelmed you? What about the scene made you feel that way?

4. The Queen of Sheba said of Solomon, "How happy your people must be! How happy your officials, who continually stand before you and hear your wisdom! Praise be to the Lord your God, who has delighted in you and placed you on the throne of Israel." Why would God have delighted in Solomon? What do you think caused Solomon to stop looking to God for wisdom?

5. How can we avoid the kinds of pitfalls that ultimately brought Solomon down?

THIRTY-TWO

Noah's Wife

*I have set my rainbow in the clouds,
and it will be the sign of the covenant
between me and the earth.*

GENESIS 9:13

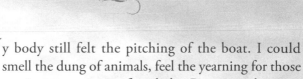

M y body still felt the pitching of the boat. I could smell the dung of animals, feel the yearning for those precious warm rays of sunlight. But more than any memory, I could still hear the screams of the people. Noah and I prayed that repentance would be on their lips, as their angry and fearsome shouts were covered over by the waters, and their souls taken before the judgment of God.

Every creature that had the breath of life in its nostrils drowned—all that were not on the ark—as the springs of the great deep burst forth and the floodgates of the heavens opened. Even the mountains were buried under the floodwaters. All perished. All land became sea. Our home and all that we had known was replaced with the rising deep and unspeakable terror.

The earth had been vanquished, washed clean of its evil, for man had lusted after all that was wicked in the sight of God. Their speech was foul as they schemed and plotted their iniquitous deeds. And I knew in my soul that the earth had been filled with the fallen tears of God.

I stirred the stew that bubbled over the open fire. Storm clouds darkened the horizon, and thunder growled from the sky. It rumbled and roared just beyond Ararat, the mountain where our ark had come to rest. The sound and smell of rain sent tremors through me. But no rain came. Instead, arcs of color slowly appeared in the clouds as if God's own finger painted the sky. Such splendorous colors, such glorious hues, illuminated by the light of heaven!

Noah called to me from the vineyards in the valley below, "Naamah!"

I ran to my husband and joined him between the rows of grapes, but my eyes never left the sky for fear the image might disappear.

"My beloved," he said to me, "this is the sign from God that I have waited for. His covenant to us, to all mankind, that he will never again destroy the earth with a flood."

"Praise him above all . . . for his promises endure forever," I said. And I felt the fear within me fade away.

Noah wrapped his arm around me as we gazed at this silent song of color and beauty, this shout of grace and glory, this mighty wonderment from God.

As witnesses of this new covenant and as stewards of this new earth, I pondered over our lives. What might our tasks be, and where would we dwell? How would we live and grow as a people? I knew not. But this I held tightly to—we would place our trust in the One who carried us away from evil, who sustained us on treacherous waters, who landed us without harm against the mountain, and then brought us safely into the new world.

"I now give you everything." Those were the words God had spoken to my husband. I filled my eyes with the sign in the sky and prayed that we would prove worthy of the task the Lord had given us.

The Story from God's Word

Genesis 9:12-17

And God said, "This is the sign of the covenant I am making between me and you and every living creature with you, a covenant for all generations to come: I have set my rainbow in the clouds, and it will be the sign of the covenant between me and the earth. Whenever I bring clouds over the earth and the rainbow appears in the clouds, I will remember my covenant between me and you and all living creatures of every kind. Never again will the waters become a flood to destroy all life. Whenever the rainbow appears in the clouds, I will see it and remember the everlasting covenant between God and all living creatures of every kind on the earth."

So God said to Noah, "This is the sign of the covenant I have established between me and all life on the earth."

THE STORY—FROM THEN TO NOW

The story of Noah and the ark has always been one of the most spectacularly dramatic stories of the Bible. It's so intense and devastating and miraculous, it's easy to run out of adjectives to describe it. On one level we cannot fathom such evil in men or such sweeping destruction, and yet when we watch the evening news we can get a pretty intense view of disaster and suffering—both natural and manmade.

> *We can still know God's mercies in all their many hues.*

But even in the midst of misfortune, we can still see beauty. Noah and his family lived the daily horror of evil and then the frightening hours of the flood, but they also got the first glorious glimpse of the rainbow—God's covenant to man.

Today, we can catch glimpses of paradise, even when the floods of suffering keep coming, and there seems to be no end in sight. Even when grief or disappointment or failure or loss has blurred our vision with tears, we can still know God's mercies in all their many hues. I like to call them remnants of Eden. They are in the heroes who rise in the midst of tragedy. They are in the drops of rain after a long drought. They are in the love and forgiveness that can come from the ashes of man's iniquity. They are in the godly men and women who choose to flee from evil—like Noah and his family. We can still witness that rainbow of divine promise. We can still know and live hope every day of our lives.

✌ THE STORY ✌
QUESTIONS TO THINK ABOUT

1. As a child, do you remember the first time you saw a rainbow? What were your thoughts and questions?

2. What do you think went through the minds of Noah and his family when they first saw God's bow in the sky?

3. Considering the ordeal they had just been through, what significance do you think the rainbow had for Noah and his family? What would it have meant to them to live in covenant with God?

4. Noah and his family saw the earth washed clean of its evil, but it did not seem to take long before man was staining the soil again. Some days it is hard to imagine that life after the flood is much different from life before with respect to the evil done by mankind. Why do you think God promised not to flood the earth again? Do you think God expected his creation to fail him again? Why or why not?

5. Even in the midst of evil and hardship and sin, we can still see beauty and hope every day—glimpses of heaven—that show us God's love for his creation. Think about some examples (other than the rainbow) of hope you have seen in the middle of scenes of suffering. How do images of hope impact your life?

6. You would think that going through such an experience and hearing the direct promise of God would be a strong motivator toward living a righteous life. What experiences have really inspired you to live life as a follower of Christ?

THIRTY-THREE

Hosea

Love her as the Lord loves the Israelites,
though they turn to other gods.

HOSEA 3:1

My wife is loved by another.** Gomer, my beloved, had been unfaithful in every way, in every word uttered from her beautiful, painted lips.

My spirit collapsed, but out of the wind, God spoke to me. Like a whispering breeze through the sycamore leaves, I heard him say, "Go show your love to your wife again, though she is loved by another man and is an adulteress. Love her as I love the Israelites, though they turn to other gods and love the sacred raisin cakes."

The tales of my wife's deeds and the news of where she lived with her lover had come back to me. So, on one warm morning in summer, just at the break of day, I entered the house where she stayed and walked to the room where I knew she slept. I saw that her lover was with her, but my gaze moved instead to my wife.

The room offered little light and the air held the stench of sweat and perfume. Gomer was naked, and as she awakened, her stare became brazen, without shame or blush—just as my countrymen were before the Almighty. I understood why God had chosen Gomer for me. I took the depth of meaning in my soul and was content with it. For God's plan had created in me a love and desperation for the salvation of my wife, which was the way I was meant to feel toward my fellow Israelites as well.

But on this morning, staring into the hard, kohl-lined eyes of my children's mother, I felt my stomach churn. She was like a piece of rotting fruit, still beautiful on the outside, but full of waste and sickness beneath her skin.

And so it will be with the Israelites, God's beloved.

"I knew you would find me," Gomer sighed. She gathered her clothes and dressed in silence.

I poked the man to rouse him from his slumber. His eyes opened and fell on the pouch I held out to him. He never met my gaze as I spoke. "Fifteen shekels of silver are in here. Take them, and the homer and lethek of barley I have left on the wagon outside your gate." I saw a glimmer of surprise pass over his face—the bounty was far more than he would have dared to ask for—then he sat up and grabbed the bag. Snatching his robes, he turned his back on us and strode out of the room. *Probably finding a place to hide his stash.*

I then turned my attention back to Gomer. "You are to live with me many days. You must not be a prostitute or be intimate with any man, and I will behave the same toward you."

Gomer took in my resolute expression, my unyielding promise, my genuine forgiveness, and slowly she gave me a nod of assent.

The desire within me was to condemn her for her sin, to march her through the streets, to make a spectacle of her disgrace. I wanted her to feel the shame she deserved to feel, to know the depth of her betrayal. And yet, she was my wife.

I knew what God was saying to me. My love needed to cover over my anger, like a mantle of snow over the dung of animals. In spite of the betrayal, I would be like one who lifts a little child to his cheek, and bends down to feed her. I would lead her with cords of human kindness, with ties of love. So it was with God and his people, even though they had played the harlot and chased after pagan gods.

I reached out to Gomer and placed her hand in mine. Her fingers felt cold and stiff, and I grasped them tighter. I did not let go. "I love you, and I still want you to be mine," I said to her.

Gomer came trembling to me, bowing her head. "We shall go home," she whispered.

And so it will be with the Israelites, God's beloved.

THE STORY FROM GOD'S WORD
HOSEA 3:1-3; 2:19, 20; 11:4

The Lord said to me, "Go, show your love to your wife again, though she is loved by another man and is an adulteress. Love her as the Lord loves the Israelites, though they turn to other gods and love the sacred raisin cakes."

So I bought her for fifteen shekels of silver and about a homer and a lethek of barley. Then I told her, "You are to live with me many days; you must not be a prostitute or be intimate with any man, and I will behave the same way toward you."

I will betroth you to me forever;
*   I will betroth you in righteousness and justice,*
*   in love and compassion.*
I will betroth you in faithfulness,
*   and you will acknowledge the Lord.*

I led them with cords of human kindness, with ties of love.
To them I was like one who lifts
*   a little child to the cheek,*
*   and I bent down to feed them.*

THE STORY—FROM THEN TO NOW
The attributes of God can be seen clearly in the Bible, and yet God is also full of great and profound mysteries. Even though we

are made in his image and we give and receive love, we cannot fathom the Creator's love for his creation. It is beyond anything that our hearts can know, especially in our fallen state.

And yet God gives us a view of his infinite love through the book of Hosea—a dual story with a unique and powerful message. God asked his prophet Hosea to marry a promiscuous woman, which at first glance seems more than a little odd, but then we read what the Israelites were up to spiritually. There is a poignant connection. The Israelites had become like a prostitute before God, worshiping other gods and getting embroiled in the detestable rituals of human sacrifice. But in spite of the grievous offenses, God chose to woo Israel, to cherish her.

Just like the Israelites, today we too have been unfaithful in every way. Our stare is brazen, without shame or blush, and it surely breaks the heart of our Lord.

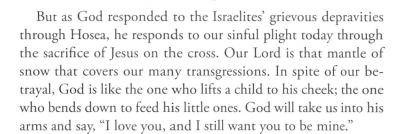

We cannot fathom the Creator's love for his creation.

But as God responded to the Israelites' grievous depravities through Hosea, he responds to our sinful plight today through the sacrifice of Jesus on the cross. Our Lord is that mantle of snow that covers our many transgressions. In spite of our betrayal, God is like the one who lifts a child to his cheek; the one who bends down to feed his little ones. God will take us into his arms and say, "I love you, and I still want you to be mine."

❧ THE STORY ❧
QUESTIONS TO THINK ABOUT

1. The Lord said to Hosea, "Go, show your love to your wife again, though she is loved by another man and is an adulteress." In that culture, an unfaithful wife was as good as dead, and brought dishonor on her whole household. What would taking her back

mean for Hosea? What emotions do you think he would ha[ve] been feeling about this challenge from God?

2. Do you see the connection between Hosea's wife and Israe[l]? God could have used any means to reach his people throug[h] the prophet Hosea. Why do you think God chose such a unique and earthly way to show Israel (and us) his anger toward idolatry, as well as his infinite mercy and love?

3. In Hosea 2, God says, "Therefore I am now going to allure her; I will lead her into the wilderness and speak tenderly to her. There I will give her back her vineyards, and will make the Valley of Achor a door of hope." How do those verses make you feel about God?

4. The Valley of Achor means the Valley of Trouble—it was the place where disobedient Achan and all his family were stoned to death (see Joshua 7). What does it mean to you that God can make a place of death into an entrance for hope?

5. Read the whole book of Hosea to get a fuller picture of God's response toward rebellion and his extravagant compassion as he tries again and again to bring his beloved back into his embrace. What truths can you discover in these chapters?

6. What part of this story is the most moving to you? What parts are the hardest to understand?

7. Some Scriptures, like those in the book of Hosea, can seem difficult to understand at first, and we may wonder how they apply to our lives today. What has helped you understand the message God has for you in this story?

THIRTY-FOUR

Jonathan

He loved him as he loved himself.
1 SAMUEL 20:17

avid drew near the palace on foot. At the sight of him, my heart felt severed in two. My father's fear of David grew more and more each day. How could I choose between my father and a loyal friend? It was an unbearable and impossible charge!

My friend approached me—in the place we had arranged to meet in secret. Anguish dimmed David's usual jaunty timbre. "What have I done?" he asked. "What is my crime? How have I wronged your father, that he is trying to kill me?"

"Never!" I replied. "You are not going to die! Look, my father doesn't do anything, great or small, without letting me know. Why would he hide this from me? It isn't so!"

But David took an oath and then said to me, "Your father knows very well that I have found favor in your eyes, and he has said to himself, 'Jonathan must not know this or he will be grieved.' Yet as surely as the Lord lives and as you live, there is only a step between me and death."

I gripped David's arm and said, "Whatever you want me to do, I'll do for you."

He pulled me into the shadows and replied, "Look, tomorrow is the New Moon feast, and I am supposed to dine with the king; but let me go and hide in the field until the evening of the day after tomorrow. If your father misses me at all, tell him, 'David earnestly asked my permission to hurry to Bethlehem, his hometown, because an annual sacrifice is being made there for his whole clan.' If he says, 'Very well,' then your servant is safe. But if he loses his temper, you can be sure that he is determined to harm me. As for you, show kindness to your servant, for you have brought him into a covenant with you before the Lord. If I am guilty, then kill me yourself! Why hand me over to your father?"

"Never!" I said to him. David motioned to me to keep my voice down, and I whispered, "If I had the least inkling that my father was determined to harm you, wouldn't I tell you?" But even as the words left my mouth, I remembered my father's erratic actions in recent days. He was not himself—it was as if . . . as if an evil spirit was on him. I could not explain it, but I no longer trusted him.

David went silent for a moment as he ran his fingers along the sharp edges of the wall, the stones stained with age and decay. He asked, "Who will tell me if your father answers you harshly?"

Whatever you want me to do, I'll do for you.

Perhaps my father felt more than fear of David and meant to harm my friend. I remembered David's victory over Goliath. The women of Israel had celebrated in the streets, dancing and singing, "Saul has slain his thousands, and David his tens of thousands." My father had gone into a rage when he heard about it.

"Come," I said. Suddenly fearful, I surveyed our surroundings. "Let us go out into the field where we can speak, and no ear can hear us."

When we walked out to the field together, I said to David, "I swear by the Lord, the God of Israel, that I will surely sound out my father by this time the day after tomorrow! If my father intends to harm you, may the Lord deal with me, be it ever so severely, if I do not let you know and send you away in peace. May the Lord be with you as he has been with my father. But show me unfailing kindness like the Lord's kindness as long as I live, so that I may not be killed, and do not ever cut off your kindness from my family—not even when the Lord has cut off every one of David's enemies from the face of the earth." I met David's eyes with mine, and I knew then he would not betray me.

So, I made a covenant with my friend and brother, David, saying, "May the Lord call David's enemies to account." And then out of love for him, I had David reaffirm his oath.

THE STORY FROM GOD'S WORD

1 SAMUEL 20:1-4

Then David fled from Naioth at Ramah and went to Jonathan and asked, "What have I done? What is my crime? How have I wronged your father, that he is trying to kill me?"

"Never!" Jonathan replied. "You are not going to die! Look, my father doesn't do anything, great or small, without letting me know. Why would he hide this from me? It isn't so!"

But David took an oath and said, "Your father knows very well that I have found favor in your eyes, and he has said to himself, 'Jonathan must not know this or he will be grieved.' Yet as surely as the Lord lives and as you live, there is only a step between me and death."

Jonathan said to David, "Whatever you want me to do, I'll do for you."

THE STORY—FROM THEN TO NOW

When you read all the biblical passages about the friendship between Jonathan and David, it's impossible not to be moved by their bond.

We all long for that kind of friendship, don't we? A friend who is fiercely loyal—someone you can call at 3:00 a.m. because you know that person is there for you in your hour of trouble.

Someone who always has your back. If you have even one friend like this, then you are fortunate indeed. But even the finest and most faithful friend will let you down eventually. It is inevitable.

It's in those moments—even though painful—that we see more clearly there is only One who will never turn his back on us. Jesus will rise above the most generous human intentions and the most ardent sacrificial deeds. Jesus knows our every need. He can be called on not only at 3:00 a.m. but every minute of every day, even when our hearts are breaking and the whole world no longer seems to care. Jesus is the one friend who will always have our backs.

❧ THE STORY ☙
QUESTIONS TO THINK ABOUT

1. David is in a desperate situation. He's innocent, and yet King Saul is trying to kill him. Jonathan says to David, "Whatever you want me to do, I'll do for you." Considering King Saul is Jonathan's father, what kind of friendship and commitment does his promise reveal to us?

2. David and Jonathan offer us a beautiful example of brotherly friendship. Do you have one or more friends who are as close to you as David was to Jonathan? In what ways have you been a support to each other in the past?

3. Lifetime friendships are not formed in a day. What are some actions that are signs of a good friend in your mind? What are the kinds of experiences that help build lasting friendships?

4. Even the best friends will let us down and sometimes hurt us. What is your best advice for mending damaged relationships?

5. Jonathan felt torn between loyalty to his father and his king and his love for his friend. Have you ever been divided between loyalties like this? What did you do?

6. Jesus is the only friend who will never fail us, not now or in eternity. How does having Christ as a friend make you a better friend to others?

THIRTY-FIVE

The Woman of Samaria

*Sir, give me this water so that
I won't get thirsty.*
JOHN 4:15

Men have fixed their gaze on me since my youth. Their eyes have always been full of desire and possessiveness. Once they owned me, though, jealousy would tear at their spirits like the talons of a lion. I have seen the blackest places of a man's heart, and that darkness clings to me day and night.

Yearning for a breeze, I picked up my water pitcher, stepped out of my dusty dwelling and into the early summer light. The sun felt like hope—welcoming and warm on my face. I made my trek to Jacob's well as was my routine—in the middle of the day, when the sun was high in the sky and most of my neighbors would be inside, seeking shelter from the heat. It was my only chance to be alone, away from the demands of my lover and the disapproving stares of the townsfolk.

But I was not alone. A Jewish man was sitting by the well. He raised his gaze to me as I approached. As I got closer, I could see he appeared weary from what must have been a long journey. He looked at me closely, but not with the desire I had seen in other men. His eyes were luminous, filled with kindness—immeasurable, like the stars of the night sky. I felt struck with awe as I took the leather bucket and lowered it into the well by its rope.

The stranger asked, "Will you give me a drink?"

As kind as he seemed, did he dare speak to a woman in public? And a Samaritan? I daubed at the sweat on my brow and answered him, "You are a Jew, and I am a Samaritan. How can you ask me for a drink?" *We Samaritans are foolish in your eyes—a cursed people!*

The stranger answered me, "If you knew the gift of God and who it is that asks you for a drink, you would have asked him and he would have given you living water."

Water that is living? I glanced at the man's face. He didn't seem unsound in his mind. . . . I was curious. "Sir, you have nothing to draw with and the well is deep. Where can you get this living water?" I kept my eyes on the rope as I pulled the full bucket back up from the well. "Are you greater than our father Jacob, who gave us the well and drank from it himself, as did also his sons and his livestock?"

The man grasped the rim of the bucket. "Everyone who drinks this water will be thirsty again, but whoever drinks the water I give them will never thirst. Indeed, the water I give them will become in them a spring of water welling up to eternal life."

The air crackled with his astonishing words. I did not know what to think, but I decided to go along with his story. With a smile, I replied, "Sir, give me this water so that I won't get thirsty and have to keep coming here to draw water."

His next words sent a chill through me. "Go, call your husband and come back."

"I have no husband," I said in a whisper. Having filled my pitcher, I turned as if to go.

The man nodded, looking past me at the village houses. "You are right when you say you have no husband. The fact is, you have had five husbands, and the man you now have is not your husband. What you have just said is quite true."

How could he know such things! My face flushed hot, not from the sun, but from the man's piercing truth. I gathered my thoughts as I set my pitcher down again on the stone ledge—I felt weak and dizzy. Perhaps I could turn his attentions away from my wayward life. "Sir," I said, "I can see that you are a prophet. Our ancestors worshiped on this mountain, but you Jews claim that the place where we must worship is in Jerusalem."

He waved a hand in front of his face—was he hiding a smile? "Woman," he replied, "believe me, a time is coming when you will worship the Father neither on this mountain nor in Jerusalem. You Samaritans worship what you do not know; we worship what we do know, for salvation is from the Jews. Yet a time is coming and has now come when the true worshipers will worship the Father in the Spirit and in truth, for they are the kind of worshipers the Father seeks. God is spirit, and his worshipers must worship in the Spirit and in truth."

His words tumbled through my mind. Who was this man? Who was this Jewish man who spoke with such authority, and brightened even the noonday sun with his knowledge of life and of God? Who was this stranger who knew everything about me and yet spoke to me with respect and kindness?

I said, "I know that the Messiah is coming. When he comes, he will explain everything to us."

Then Jesus declared, "I, the one speaking to you—I am he."

The Story from God's Word
John 4:7-14, 25, 26

When a Samaritan woman came to draw water, Jesus said to her, "Will you give me a drink?" (His disciples had gone into the town to buy food.)

The Samaritan woman said to him, "You are a Jew and I am a Samaritan woman. How can you ask me for a drink?" (For Jews do not associate with Samaritans.)

Jesus answered her, "If you knew the gift of God and who it is that asks you for a drink, you would have asked him and he would have given you living water."

"Sir," the woman said, "you have nothing to draw with and the well is deep. Where can you get this living water? Are you greater than our father Jacob, who gave us the well and drank from it himself, as did also his sons and his livestock?"

Jesus answered, "Everyone who drinks this water will be thirsty again, but whoever drinks the water I give them will never thirst. Indeed, the water I give them will become in them a spring of water welling up to eternal life."

The woman said, "I know that Messiah" (called Christ) "is coming. When he comes, he will explain everything to us."

Then Jesus declared, "I, the one speaking to you—I am he."

THE STORY—FROM THEN TO NOW

The Samaritan woman at the well was most likely an outcast among her people, since she lived with a man, unmarried. She must have also felt loneliness in her transgressions. Even without succumbing to her particular sin, we can all know that feeling of being outside the circle.

In high school there were many times I felt outside that communal orbit. I was a misfit, stumbling around verbally, athletically, socially—feeling as though I were on the outside of a pretty snow globe while everyone else was tucked inside, having a ball. Back then, life was a strain, trying to squeeze my square personality into a round world. At times I still feel the same way. Perhaps you do too.

> *We can all know that feeling of being outside the circle.*

As Christians, we can sometimes get that same "odd one out" kind of feeling. But we will never truly fit in here. Nor should we. This fallen earth in its current state is not our final destination. We are sojourners on a road to another life. But in heaven, we will no longer feel like we're merely passing through. We won't carry that ache of being an outcast, wondering where we belong. We will know intimately what Jesus meant when he talked about a spring of water welling up to eternal life. We will take in the Son's light, warm on our faces. We will drink from the living water and never be thirsty. And we will hear the air crackle with his mighty voice, "Welcome home!"

✢ THE STORY ✢
QUESTIONS TO THINK ABOUT

1. The woman of Samaria was used to being an object rather than a beloved woman. How would you describe the way Jesus treated her?

2. The Samaritan woman was full of questions. I would be too, especially if I found out the man I was speaking to was the Messiah. What do you think was her goal in asking the questions she asked?

3. The woman of Samaria said, "I know that Messiah" (called Christ) "is coming. When he comes, he will explain everything to us." Jesus didn't avoid her question; he stated clearly that he was the Messiah. But at other times Jesus was vague about his identity. Why do you think he was sometimes elusive about who he was? Why do you think he made himself known to this woman?

4. Can you relate to the way this Samaritan woman must have viewed herself? Why or why not?

5. For each of us, there are things in our past we would rather forget or be rid of completely. What do you think Jesus sees when he looks at you? How can you move on from your past and become a new creation in Christ?

6. Think of all the ways the Samaritan woman could have been thirsty. How could knowing Jesus fill her up and quench her thirst?

7. Jesus talks to the woman about different kinds of water and about different kinds of worship. What do you think it means to worship in the Spirit and in truth?

THIRTY-SIX

Stephen

"Look," he said, "I see heaven open and the Son of Man standing at the right hand of God."

ACTS 7:56

The members of the Sanhedrin writhed under my rebuking words, but I did not temper my speech, since I was sure of the source of my authority. I raised my hands, and through the power of the Holy Spirit, I continued my scalding denunciations, "You people are stiff-necked! Your hearts and ears are still uncircumcised. You are just like your ancestors. You always resist the Holy Spirit. Was there ever a prophet your ancestors did not persecute? They even killed those who predicted the coming of the Righteous One. And now you have betrayed and murdered him, you who have received the law that was given through angels but have not obeyed it."

When the members of the Sanhedrin heard this, they were furious and gnashed their teeth at me.

I gazed up to heaven and saw the glory of God. "Look," I said to them, "I see heaven open and the Son of Man standing at the right hand of God."

At this they covered their ears, and, yelling at the top of their voices, they all rushed at me and pushed me to the ground. My

accusers spewed accusations. They grabbed at my clothes—
someone caught hold of my arms and bent them behind me. I
could feel them wrapping something tightly around my wrists,
then my ankles. It all happened with such haste, then I was being pulled out of the city. I caught sight of that zealot named
Saul as my head dragged on the ground. He was surrounded
by people who were laying their coats at his feet. The thought
passed through my mind that someone needed to watch him—
he was a grave threat to all who followed Christ. But it was too
late for me to warn anyone now.

The crowd pushed me into a ravine and I half fell, half slid
down the rocky wall. A man barked at me, commanding me to
get to my feet. I looked up and saw the snarling faces. One by
one, the witnesses picked up their stones.

Another man yelled, signaling the crowd. The shout echoed
through the ravine. Then they began hurling stones at me. The
rocks struck my arms and chest, searing my flesh like burning
rods.

> *One by one, the witnesses picked up their stones.*

I raised my voice to the heavens and prayed, "Lord Jesus,
receive my spirit." Instead of feeling hatred for the crowd, my
heart grieved for their souls, for they had been devoured by lies
and taken over by Satan. Bruised and exhausted, I fell on my
knees. Pain shot up my thighs and through my spine. "Lord," I
cried out, "do not hold this sin against them."

A stone struck my temple with great force, and a cheer went
up from the crowd. Blood trailed down my face making sprays
of crimson on my chest. On the earth. All around me.

I did not think of the horrors of the tomb but only of life.
And then in what seemed to be a whirlwind of light, all pain
vanished. I felt no more. My heart ceased its beating, and my
body, no longer my own, crumpled onto the dusty ground like

ancient parchment. I had come to my end on this earth. *My Lord, you are my strength and my Redeemer.*

As I drifted into what felt like mortal sleep, angels appeared, ministering to me. Then with song and rejoicing, these glorious messengers of heaven ushered me into the very presence of my Savior!

THE STORY FROM GOD'S WORD

ACTS 7:51–8:1

"You stiff-necked people! Your hearts and ears are still uncircumcised. You are just like your ancestors: You always resist the Holy Spirit! Was there ever a prophet your ancestors did not persecute? They even killed those who predicted the coming of the Righteous One. And now you have betrayed and murdered him—you who have received the law that was given through angels but have not obeyed it."

When the members of the Sanhedrin heard this, they were furious and gnashed their teeth at him. But Stephen, full of the Holy Spirit, looked up to heaven and saw the glory of God, and Jesus standing at the right hand of God. "Look," he said, "I see heaven open and the Son of Man standing at the right hand of God."

At this they covered their ears and, yelling at the top of their voices, they all rushed at him, dragged him out of the city and began to stone him. Meanwhile, the witnesses laid their coats at the feet of a young man named Saul.

While they were stoning him, Stephen prayed, "Lord Jesus, receive my spirit." Then he fell on his knees and cried out, "Lord, do not hold this sin against them." When he had said this, he fell asleep.

And Saul approved of their killing him.

THE STORY—FROM THEN TO NOW

The drama in Stephen's story reaches a feverish pitch when we realize that an innocent man is about to be stoned. Stephen is pronounced guilty, and yet he is a godly man. Saul, the man who becomes a religious zealot, killing Christians, did not partake in this hate-filled crime that day. He just gave his approval. Saul (who later became the apostle Paul after his conversion) may not have hurled a stone at Stephen, but he did nothing to stop the crowd from killing this man.

> *You don't actually have to be throwing a stone to be party to the ending of a life.*

I cannot imagine the terror of watching someone being stoned. But there have been times when I've been silent on the sidelines as I listened to people hurl insults and gossip about other people I knew. I may not have approved of the mud that was being slung, but I did not always try to stop it. Perhaps listening and nodding is very close to the actual act of gossiping. You don't actually have to be throwing a stone to be party to the ending of a life.

Now, you might be thinking that I'm being a little extreme. Gossip isn't ranked anywhere near such a heinous crime as murder, right? But in the book of Romans (which, by the way, was written by that guy who held the coats for the people who killed Stephen), gossips are placed alongside some pretty serious sinners, such as those who "invent ways of doing evil" and "God-haters."

Oh dear.

The stones of rumor-mongering may not feel as searing to the body as the stones that killed Stephen, but gossip can still sting. It can destroy a reputation or decimate a spirit—even that of an innocent person. The tongue is a powerful instrument, able to wield a blessing or a curse—life or death. I know which ones I want to choose to produce. Pray that I follow through, and that I speak up when those rumor stones start to fly.

1. One of the charges that Stephen hurled at the Sanhedrin was this: "You always resist the Holy Spirit." Think of some examples of ways we struggle against the Holy Spirit today. When do you feel that spiritual resistance?

2. Before Stephen died, he saw heaven open and the Son of Man standing at the right hand of God. A number of my Christian relatives and friends who have now passed on spoke of seeing heavenly visions in the days leading up to their deaths. Why do you think God gave Stephen this supernatural moment before his death?

3. While Stephen was being stoned he prayed, "Lord Jesus, receive my spirit." Then he fell on his knees and cried out, "Lord, do not hold this sin against them." What does this prayer reveal about Stephen's character? What other biblical story is echoed in this scene?

4. What are some ways we can emulate the kind of faith-filled and victorious life that Stephen lived? How can we use our words boldly for Christ?

5. What do you think about the comparison of stone-throwing to gossiping? Have you ever been hurt by gossip? What happened?

6. How do you control your tongue? What tips would you give others who struggle with gossip?

THIRTY-SEVEN

Manoah

"We are doomed to die!" he said to his wife.
"We have seen God!"

JUDGES 13:22

M y wife ran toward me from the field, waving her arms and yelling. "He's here!" she said, "The man who appeared to me the other day!"

God heard my prayer. The stranger had returned! I got up, and with great haste, followed my wife to the field. When I came to the man who stood gazing at us, I inquired of him, "Are you the man who talked to my wife?"

"I am," he said.

I asked him the question I had repeated over and over in my mind. "When your words are fulfilled, what is to be the rule that governs the boy's life and work?"

The stranger answered, "Your wife must do all that I have told her. She must not eat anything that comes from the grapevine, nor drink any wine or other fermented drink nor eat anything unclean. She must do everything I have commanded her."

As the man turned to go, his robe opened briefly, revealing a garment of snow white. I wished to ask this stranger many questions. Where he had come from, and what the details were surrounding the child he had foretold—the boy my wife would bear. *Perhaps I can persuade him to remain with us a while longer.*

I implored him, "Please stay until we prepare a young goat for you."

The man turned his attention to me again. "Even though you detain me, I will not eat any of your food. But if you prepare a burnt offering, offer it to the Lord."

I could not relinquish my anxiety concerning this mysterious stranger, so I asked, "What is your name, so that we may honor you when your word comes true?"

He replied simply, "Why do you ask my name? It is beyond understanding."

I considered his reply, but could not comprehend his meaning. I said no more to him but did as he suggested. I took a young goat from the pen, and together with the grain offering, I sacrificed it on a rock.

My wife and I watched as the fire began to consume our offering. Suddenly, the flame blazed up from the altar like a column toward heaven. The heat intensified, forcing us to back away. In a blinding flash, the stranger transformed into a smoldering vapor, coiled up into the blaze, and vanished into a fissure in the clouds. Seeing this, we fell with our faces to the ground. We waited there, trembling. I realized then that the stranger was indeed an angel of the Lord.

Panic poured over me like a chilling fever, and my breath quickened into gasps. "We are doomed to die!" I said. "We have seen God!" I stood up and tore at my hair and clothes.

My wife rose, but she did not become alarmed. Instead she stared up into the heavens at the lingering hazy glow. After a few quiet moments, she laid a hand on my arm. "If the Lord had meant to kill us, he would not have accepted a burnt offering and grain offering from our hands, nor shown us all these things or now told us this."

My wife's words were true. We did not perish. Nine months later, she gave birth to a boy—Samson. He grew up to be a fine-looking and an uncommonly strong man. And the Lord blessed him. We praised the Almighty for our blessing, for our son was consecrated for God's mighty purpose among our people.

The Story from God's Word

Judges 13:1-9

Again the Israelites did evil in the eyes of the Lord, so the Lord delivered them into the hands of the Philistines for forty years.

A certain man of Zorah, named Manoah, from the clan of the Danites, had a wife who was childless, unable to give birth. The angel of the Lord appeared to her and said, "You are barren and childless, but you are going to become pregnant and give birth to a son. Now see to it that you drink no wine or other fermented drink and that you do not eat anything unclean. You will become pregnant and have a son whose head is never to be touched by a razor because the boy is to be a Nazirite, dedicated to God from the womb. He will take the lead in delivering Israel from the hands of the Philistines."

Then the woman went to her husband and told him, "A man of God came to me. He looked like an angel of God, very awesome. I didn't ask him where he came from, and he didn't tell me his name. But he said to me, 'You will become pregnant and have a son. Now then, drink no wine or other fermented drink and do not eat anything unclean, because the boy will be a Nazirite of God from the womb until the day of his death.'"

Then Manoah prayed to the Lord: "Pardon your servant, Lord. I beg you to let the man of God you sent to us come again to teach us how to bring up the boy who is to be born."

God heard Manoah, and the angel of God came again to the woman while she was out in the field; but her husband Manoah was not with her.

The Story—from Then to Now

Is it just me, or does Manoah strike you as a worrier? Let's review the story (see Judges 13). First of all, his wife receives an amazing vision with some equally amazing news—they're going to have a son!

Did you see how excited Manoah became? How he threw a party and was so happy to hear this news, after all those years of waiting for a child?

No? You didn't read that part? Me neither.

No, Manoah didn't seem to get excited. He got worried. So he asked God to send another messenger so they could get some parenting classes. Then God actually answers his prayer, and the angel of God reappears.

But Manoah is thinking too hard to even notice this is an angel. He just wants to ask his question. "What are the rules?"

Then when he finally realizes that God has sent him an angel, and gets to watch an amazing display of God's glory, all Manoah can do is think: "We're going to die!!!" I can just see his wife, shaking her head and patting Manoah's hand: "There, there, dear. We're not going to die. How could I have a baby if I'm dead?"

> *It's one of the sneakiest methods of the Enemy—*
> *twisting God's gifts to us into*
> *just another headache.*

Have you ever met someone like Manoah? Or maybe you see yourself in him? God gives you a blessing, and you can't accept it. You've got to figure out how it happened, plan for what to do with it, and worry about how you might lose it. You're so busy thinking about the thing, you forget to enjoy it. To be thankful for it. To praise God for it. And if you're not careful, you might just miss it altogether.

It's one of the sneakiest methods of the Enemy—twisting God's gifts to us into just another headache.

I am embarrassed to say how closely I can relate to Manoah's story. Recently I found myself in a heated cauldron of worry in an area of my life where God has clearly blessed me. I took my fears to God, but I admit I did some hand wringing along with the prayers. My joy was crushed, because my mind was occupied on every possible negative scenario and how my situation could spiral into disaster. Jesus said, "Can any one of you by worrying add a single hour to your life?" (Matthew 6:27).

Don't get me a wrong. There's definitely a time for planning and thinking about things. But there's also a time to celebrate. Let's not let the Enemy steal even a second of the joy God gives us!

✻ THE STORY ✻
QUESTIONS TO THINK ABOUT

1. A lot of churches offer baby dedications these days, but I don't see many having womb dedication services. Manoah's' wife was told her baby would be "dedicated to God from the womb." How do you think these words affected her? How would such a message affect you?

2. Raising children is a pretty serious undertaking—there's no doubt about it. You can't really blame Manoah for wanting to consult a higher authority for advice. Manoah asks an interesting question: "What is to be the rule that governs the boy's life and work?" What rule would you say your life and work is governed by?

3. Manoah wanted the angel to stay for supper. Why do you think the angel refused the meal but stayed for Manoah's sacrifice to the Lord?

4. In the Bible we read about the angel Gabriel and the angel Michael, among others. But this angel claims his name is "beyond understanding." What is it about knowing someone's name that makes us feel closer to a person? Why do you think the angel could not give his name?

5. The story in Judges reads, "And the Lord did an amazing thing while Manoah and his wife watched: As the flame blazed up from the altar toward heaven, the angel of the Lord ascended in the flame." Why do you think the angel left their presence in such a dramatic way?

6. When Manoah misunderstood the angel's fiery departure, his wife responded with the voice of reason, saying, "If the Lord had meant to kill us, he would not have accepted a burnt offering and grain offering from our hands, nor shown us all these things or now told us this." Why do you think Manoah believed the Lord was going to kill them?

7. Manoah had many concerns—and no doubt those multiplied as Samson grew older. Is worrying a sin? Explain your answer. What effect can worry have on a person's ability to know and follow God?

THIRTY-EIGHT

Puah

The midwives, however, feared God.

EXODUS 1:17

f I displeased Pharaoh with my answer, he would throw me into prison, along with my fellow midwife, Shiphrah. Or he might choose to sentence us to death for our disobedience, even though we were blameless before God.

The moment I positioned myself before the king on his throne, he raised his scepter, and in a thundering voice, asked, "Why have you done this thing? Why have you allowed the Hebrew boys to live —against my decree?"

I fastened my hands together behind me to cease their quaking. Why did the king fear the Hebrews so? I tried to speak, but my lips betrayed me. Yet to delay my answer would place us both—Shiphrah and me—in peril.

What would the king of Egypt know of our laws? He would have no reverence or understanding for what is treasured in God's sight. He knew nothing of Hebrew families. The last birth I had attended flashed through my mind. They were a beautiful family—blessed with six children, and now one more. In fact, the mother did not even really need my help—her seventh babe came before I arrived . . .

In a burst of conviction, I finally answered, "Hebrew women are not like Egyptian woman. They are vigorous and give birth before the midwives arrive." Those in the king's court glared at me with disbelief, and Pharaoh did not appear persuaded or even swayed by my speech.

My heart fluttered and my skin crawled as I awaited the king's ruling. I felt no remorse for my actions, though, since I could not take innocent life. Only the Most High had authority over death and life.

In my dread I sought the mercy of the Almighty and prayed for deliverance. *Lord God, have mercy on your servant, who fears you and places your decrees and your sovereignty far above Pharaoh. Shiphrah and I have honored your gift of birth and life by saving your infants. Please have mercy on your servants now—the mid-wives of your beloved people—and save us from the king's wrath and judgment.*

Peace settled in my spirit like the deep waters of the Nile. Neither the pageantry of Pharaoh's opulent court, nor the flames from his torches, nor the sharp spears of his guards could threaten us—for God was on our side. Shiphrah and I were in the service of the King of kings. We would continue to assist our women, and no earthly ruler or army could thwart our duty or impede our calling!

THE STORY FROM GOD'S WORD

EXODUS 1:15-21

The king of Egypt said to the Hebrew midwives, whose names were Shiphrah and Puah, "When you are helping the Hebrew women during childbirth on the delivery stool, if you see that the baby is a boy, kill him; but if it is a girl, let her live." The midwives, however, feared God and did not do what the king of Egypt had told them to do; they let the boys live. Then the king of Egypt summoned the midwives and asked them, "Why have you done this? Why have you let the boys live?"

The midwives answered Pharaoh, "Hebrew women are not like Egyptian women; they are vigorous and give birth before the mid-wives arrive."

So God was kind to the midwives and the people increased and became even more numerous. And because the midwives feared God, he gave them families of their own.

THE STORY—FROM THEN TO NOW

The passion of conviction is honorable to see, and the two midwives in this story had plenty of it. God was so pleased with these women, in fact, he gave them families of their own. But whether in Bible times or in this modern world, conviction without truth leads to spiritual bankruptcy. Lots of people today have strong beliefs, but those persuasions may have no value. Without the truth to hold them up they are like paper novelties that get tattered in the winds of our own agendas.

Those Hebrew midwives revered the Almighty, and within that devotion to the living God they were more concerned about what he would say about taking human life than what was politically useful and self-serving for the king.

> *Conviction without truth leads to spiritual bankruptcy.*

Today, we have allowed the pagan philosophies of the ancient Egyptians to rule our world—that is, the expediency of abortion comes before the consideration of human life. We no longer care what God thinks as much as we care about what we think and what others think. We can either choose to honor the innocent life God entrusts us with, or we can terminate life when it no longer fits our agenda or meshes with our plans. Every day we make decisions of all kinds, but this one choice goes far beyond our own lives—it extends to all the many generations that would have been . . .

1. If you read Exodus 1, you'll be able to answer these questions: Why did the king of Egypt want to destroy the Hebrew baby boys? Why did the king fear the Hebrew people?

2. Concerning the midwives, Shiphrah and Puah, why did fearing God stop them from killing the newborn Hebrew boys?

3. How do you think the concept of the fear of God has changed since the days of Pharoah we read about in Exodus? Explain.

4. Exodus 1:20, 21 reads, "So God was kind to the midwives and the people increased and became even more numerous. And because the midwives feared God, he gave them families of their own." What can we learn from this passage?

5. The new king wanted to deal shrewdly with the Israelites to keep them from growing an even bigger population and to keep them from siding with an enemy. So his plans included oppressing them even more harshly and forcing them to kill their own sons. What do you think of the king's plans? Considering what happened among the Israelites subsequently, would you rate his plans as effective? Why or why not?

6. What can we learn about faith through the story of Shiphrah and Puah?

THIRTY-NINE

Bathsheba

Solomon your son shall be king after me, and
he will sit on my throne in my place.

1 KINGS 1:30

*T*he king has aged even in my brief absence. It grieved me
to see his eyes so deep set and such pallor on his cheek.
Death was growing ever nearer to his chamber, which
made troubling him as unpleasant as it was urgent! But what
other course had I been given? King David's throne had been
robbed from him and from Solomon, the future king—my son!
I had to plead for justice.

The king and I had been through many struggles through
our lives, and yet our troubles rose again like the final blows of a
battle. The name of our last war was Adonijah!

I fingered the gold necklace—a gift from the king when
Solomon was born—and it came with a pledge that one day
my son would sit on the throne of Israel and Judah. Nathan
the prophet and I had made our impassioned pleas to the king
on this very morn, and now we waited for the ruling—his
decree—in the matter. If the king did nothing, Solomon would
not take the throne, and my son and I would surely be put to
death as traitors to Adonijah.

I did not move, as I waited for the king's answer.

"Bathsheba."

The king's attendant called me back into the room. With some effort, King David raised himself up from the bed. There before me he took an oath, saying, "As surely as the Lord lives, who has delivered me out of every trouble, I will surely carry out this very day what I swore to you by the Lord, the God of Israel: Solomon your son shall be king after me, and he will sit on my throne in my place."

Praise be to the God of heaven. Adonijah may be the king's eldest now, and he may have set himself up as king, but it was never meant to stand! Since Adonijah's youth, he had always been full of deceitful ways, but now this new dark and devious scheme had been overthrown by the king. I bowed down with my face to the ground, prostrating myself before him, and said, "May my lord King David live forever!"

The king said, "Call in Zadok the priest, Nathan the prophet, and Benaiah son of Jehoiada."

I left the room when they came before the king, but I stood outside the door to listen.

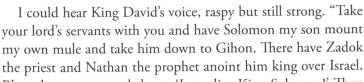

I released a deep sigh in my spirit, for now I would see the king's promise fulfilled.

I could hear King David's voice, raspy but still strong. "Take your lord's servants with you and have Solomon my son mount my own mule and take him down to Gihon. There have Zadok the priest and Nathan the prophet anoint him king over Israel. Blow the trumpet and shout, 'Long live King Solomon!' Then you are to go up with him, and he is to come and sit on my throne and reign in my place. I have appointed him ruler over Israel and Judah."

I released a deep sigh in my spirit, for now I would see the king's promise fulfilled. My son, Solomon, would be king after all. But even though the cunning Adonijah had failed at this attempt to steal the throne, I knew he would have to be watched.

With his fine stature and his position within the lineage of the king, his lust for power would surely rise again.

I rested my head against the strong, cool stone wall. Solomon was still young, but he would make a good king. He had always longed to do what was right before the Lord. I closed my eyes and remembered another time—another husband, and a child whose tiny face had all but faded from my memory.

Yes, Solomon, my beloved son—your name will be remembered for all time.

THE STORY FROM GOD'S WORD
1 KINGS 1:28-35

Then King David said, "Call in Bathsheba." So she came into the king's presence and stood before him.

The king then took an oath: "As surely as the Lord lives, who has delivered me out of every trouble, I will surely carry out this very day what I swore to you by the Lord, the God of Israel: Solomon your son shall be king after me, and he will sit on my throne in my place."

Then Bathsheba bowed down with her face to the ground, prostrating herself before the king, and said, "May my lord King David live forever!"

King David said, "Call in Zadok the priest, Nathan the prophet and Benaiah son of Jehoiada." When they came before the king, he said to them: "Take your lord's servants with you and have Solomon my son mount my own mule and take him down to Gihon. There have Zadok the priest and Nathan the prophet anoint him king over Israel. Blow the trumpet and shout, 'Long live King Solomon!' Then you are to go up with him, and he is to come and sit on my throne and reign in my place. I have appointed him ruler over Israel and Judah."

THE STORY—FROM THEN TO NOW

Humility is like a butterfly—it's so elusive that when you're certain you possess it, it may have already flitted away. In the story, Adonijah, Solomon's rival for the throne, had very little of this trait. He was handsome and overly confident, and he felt he deserved to be king, even without his father's endorsement.

It's easy to become full of ourselves like Adonijah—thinking we deserve to be king in our sphere of influence. But in the Bible, pride is not only frowned upon, it's detested. Proverbs says that a haughty spirit comes before a fall. Surely this is a lesson King David would have been familiar with. In fact, when God delivered him from the hand of Saul, David sang these words (2 Samuel 22:28): "You save the humble, but your eyes are on the haughty to bring them low."

Recently I went to a get-together where I thought I would be honored, but in the end, the event was more service-related than it was about showcasing me. By the end of the evening, I felt disappointed and even a little cheated. But then I realized that my attitude was diva-like and was probably not pleasing to the Lord. God is more impressed with my graciousness than my grandstanding.

> *Humility is like a butterfly—it's so elusive that when you're certain you possess it, it may have already flitted away.*

It's easy to think that we deserve to sit at the head table of life. But Jesus says this:

> When someone invites you to a wedding feast, do not take the place of honor, for a person more distinguished than you may have been invited. If so, the host who invited both of you will come and say to you, 'Give this person your seat.' Then, humiliated, you will have to take the least important place. But when you are invited, take the lowest place, so that when your host comes, he will say to you, 'Friend, move up to a better place.' Then you will be honored in the presence of all the other guests. For all those who exalt themselves will be humbled, and those who humble themselves will be exalted. (Luke 14:8-11)

That passage summarizes the spirit of humility perfectly, which is as beautiful and precious to gaze upon as a bride on her wedding day.

For Solomon, taking his place as king was not about pride, but promise. The position had been promised to him, and it was a promise his father would not break.

✒ THE STORY ✒
QUESTIONS TO THINK ABOUT

1. When King David heard that Adonijah tried to pronounce himself king instead of his son, Solomon, David took an oath: "As surely as the Lord lives, who has delivered me out of every trouble, I will surely carry out this very day what I swore to you by the Lord, the God of Israel: Solomon your son shall be king after me, and he will sit on my throne in my place." Why did David want Solomon on the throne?

2. Why do you think God wanted Solomon on the throne?

3. How did God work with Bathsheba to fulfill his plan?

4. David said an oath that day concerning his son, Solomon. Why do you think these verbal pledges were so important in Bible times?

5. Why would God allow Solomon to be on the throne when he knew that his reign would eventually end in spiritual defeat?

FORTY

$Simeon$

You may now dismiss your servant in peace.
For my eyes have seen your salvation.
LUKE 2:29, 30

Sensing an urgency from the Spirit of God to enter the
temple courts, I did so at once. A young couple with
an infant had just entered. They must have come to
Jerusalem to consecrate their firstborn son to the Lord. When the
parents approached me with the child, and I took him in my arms,
I knew—I had seen the face of the Messiah!

Praising God, I said, "Sovereign Lord, as you have promised,
you may now dismiss your servant in peace. For my eyes have
seen your salvation, which you have prepared in the sight of all
nations: a light for revelation to the Gentiles, and the glory of
your people Israel."

The child's mother and father, Mary and Joseph, gaped in
wonder at all I said, yet surely they knew he was the anointed
one. I pronounced a blessing on the child and on his parents.
As I handed him back to his mother, the holy infant cooed like
a dove.

I looked in Mary's eyes. "This child is destined to cause the
falling and rising of many in Israel, and to be a sign that will
be spoken against, so that the thoughts of many hearts will be
revealed. And a sword will pierce your own soul too." A shadow

passed over the young girl's face, but she nodded her head and murmured a word of thanks. I knew my words must surely cause the child's mother some pain to hear them, and yet I knew the prophecy to be true.

Anna, a prophetess and the daughter of Penuel, of the tribe of Asher, also came to see the baby and give her blessing. Anna was very old and had spent most of her years as a widow. She never left the temple, but worshiped night and day, fasting and praying. I watched as Anna laid hands on the child and gave thanks to God. Then she spoke about the child to all those around us who were looking forward to the redemption of Jerusalem.

When the young parents had done everything required by the Law of the Lord, they returned to Galilee, to their own town of Nazareth.

I watched them go that day until their figures disappeared on the horizon. Then I returned to my own chamber, for I knew my time had come. I lay down and closed my eyes, knowing peace. I could see the Christ child in my mind, growing strong and becoming filled with wisdom. The grace of God was on him wherever he went. And the world, the whole of the world, would never be the same again.

THE STORY FROM GOD'S WORD
LUKE 2:27-40

Moved by the Spirit, he went into the temple courts. When the parents brought in the child Jesus to do for him what the custom of the Law required, Simeon took him in his arms and praised God, saying:

> *"Sovereign Lord, as you have promised,*
> *you may now dismiss your servant in peace.*
> *For my eyes have seen your salvation,*
> *which you have prepared in the sight of all nations:*
> *a light for revelation to the Gentiles,*
> *and the glory of your people Israel."*

The child's father and mother marveled at what was said about him. Then Simeon blessed them and said to Mary, his mother: "This child is destined to cause the falling and rising of many in Israel, and to be a sign that will be spoken against, so that the thoughts of many hearts will be revealed. And a sword will pierce your own soul too."

There was also a prophet, Anna, the daughter of Penuel, of the tribe of Asher. She was very old; she had lived with her husband seven years after her marriage, and then was a widow until she was eighty-four. She never left the temple but worshiped night and day, fasting and praying. Coming up to them at that very moment, she gave thanks to God and spoke about the child to all who were looking forward to the redemption of Jerusalem.

When Joseph and Mary had done everything required by the Law of the Lord, they returned to Galilee to their own town of Nazareth. And the child grew and became strong; he was filled with wisdom, and the grace of God was on him.

> *Imagine how he must have felt as he held the Messiah he had been waiting for.*

The Story—from Then to Now

When the prophet Simeon viewed the infant in his arms, he knew he was holding a living miracle. He was staring into the face of God! Imagine how he must have felt as he held the Messiah he had been waiting for.

This prophetic story in Luke also reads, "And the child grew and became strong; he was filled with wisdom, and the grace of God was on him." Jesus was a man, and he is God, and he came into this world to love us into his kingdom. To give us life in place of death. To give us that paradise lost. If you have not yet looked into the face of Christ and seen him as your Savior and as the Son of the only God—the only One who can offer you real peace and joy and hope and love and grace enough to cover all your sins, I ask you to pray about this. And if you know him as your Savior, but perhaps have forgotten your joy or turned away from God's love, I challenge you to read the stories about him again and again. Step into the pages of the Bible and take the Christ child in your arms. Look into his face and find peace again—the same peace that came to Simeon.

Every year, much of the world still takes a day to remember and talk about and celebrate that peace. Jesus' birthday—his coming into our world—was a hallowed and glorious event. I can imagine that night sky lit with God's glory and the thunderous adorations of the heavenly host; it must have been electrifying! Serious rejoicing took place on earth and in the heavens—it was the kind of awe-inspiring event no one could be silent about.

Jesus' arrival still has the same sacred and exciting significance today, which should make us want to bubble up with the words, "Merry Christmas!" Just as the angels in heaven and the shepherds were praising God over Jesus' birth, we should share our happy acknowledgments of the occasion with our whole being, so that our faces reflect the magnificence and gladness of the season. Our hearts should leap and shout like the rejuvenated and reformed Scrooge on Christmas morning.

Some in this world may want to quiet us—they want to remove the reminders of Christ from the celebration of the most life-altering event in human history. But we should not be silent. Whether it be in the temple courts, the church pews, the store aisles, or the city centers, we should never allow anyone to smother our joy or our words, for Christmas brings us the only peace and hope this hurting world will ever know.

THE STORY
Questions to Think About

1. Luke 2:22 reads, "When the time came for the purification rites required by the Law of Moses, Joseph and Mary took him to Jerusalem to present him to the Lord (as it is written in the Law of the Lord, "Every firstborn male is to be consecrated to the Lord"), and to offer a sacrifice in keeping with what is said in the Law of the Lord: "a pair of doves or two young pigeons."

Why do you think Jesus' parents fulfilled these requirements of the Law?

2. Simeon took the baby Jesus in his arms and praised God, saying, "Sovereign Lord, as you have promised, you may now dismiss your servant in peace." Why do you think it was so important that Simeon see the Messiah before he died?

3. Simeon said to Jesus' mother, "And a sword will pierce your own soul too." Imagine you are Mary, hearing those words. How would you feel?

4. This biblical scene also tells us that there was another prophet at the scene. Anna never left the temple but worshiped night and day, fasting and praying. It would be hard to duplicate Anna's devotion today, but what are some realistic steps we can take to be more disciplined in the growing of our faith and in our worship?

5. Have you acknowledged that the child of Mary and Joseph is also the Son of God and came to save you from your sins? If not, what is holding you back? If you have, how are you telling others about this amazing story?

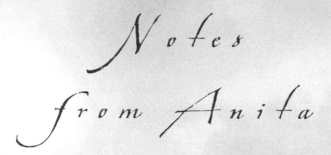

Notes from Anita

Writing biblical fiction is not an easy undertaking. In fact, the strain of it reminded me of Jesus' word picture of the camel going through the eye of a needle. It requires considerable research and plenty of rewrites. One of my goals in this book was to weave the fictional segments seamlessly into the existing biblical fabric. I also wanted to make the scenes come to life. For instance, when we journeyed to the Kerith Ravine to see Elijah fed by the ravens, I wanted you to see the way their wings shimmered in the dawn; I wanted you to hear their musical cries and their wings beating, swiftly and softly. I'll let you, the reader, decide if I accomplished these difficult tasks.

During the months of research as well as the writing of this book, I held to the routine of listening to the Scriptures on CDs—in my car running errands or getting ready in the morning. I did this hoping to absorb the Bible's rich language, dramatic metaphors, and epic tone. On some days the words flowed with little effort, almost like taking dictation, and on other days I struggled to complete one or two pages. But amidst my routine and with an aching back from long hours at the computer, the one thing that helped me more than anything was prayer. God really was faithful in helping me prepare this devotional book.

To give you a view that's more personal, I will mention that during the months I wrote this manuscript, I was fighting to stay afloat on the unstable waters of menopause, empty nest, the helpless frustration of watching one of my relatives battle with cancer, and a curious array of my own health issues that doctors said were stress related.

I'm sure you've endured your own storms in this life. As you discovered in this book, no matter the time period, we all face rough seas. We may not walk on water and cry out like Peter did, but the story still rings true today—with our artificial bravado, our relentless doubts and fears, and our faith tossed to and fro. But all of us, people in both ancient and modern times, have this intense yearning to finish well. To call out to the Lord and not sink, to not be pulled under by the swells and surges of life.

I pray this devotional book gives you new hope in riding out those storms. As you walk alongside the ancient Bible characters, as you see their travails, their profound humanness, and their inextinguishable love for God, my desire is that by observing their trials, you would gain fresh insight into your own, and that these stories would infuse you with calm, stir you with change, and bring you the peace that only Christ can give.

Through the writing of these devotions I sensed the Holy Spirit whispering, "This book is going to change your life, Anita." And now as I'm typing the last words of this manuscript, I have to admit that it did. Even though all my troubles didn't vanish when I finished the last page, I did come away with clarity, aware that the same God who set the stars in the heavens also knows the number of hairs on my head. Jesus is nearer than I imagined and cares more than I'd hoped. And he's constantly working things out for good in my life. And in your life . . .

I'll close with this lovely Irish blessing, which has always been a favorite of mine:
> May the road rise to meet you,
> May the wind be always at your back.
> May the sun shine warm upon your face,

The rains fall soft upon your fields.

And until we meet again,

May God hold you in the palm of his hand.

If this book impacted your life in some way I'd love to hear from you. And if it didn't, I'd still love to hear from you. You're welcome to e-mail me through the "contact me" button on my website at www.anitahigman.com.

Best-selling and award-winning author, Anita Higman, has thirty books published (several coauthored) for adults and children. She's been a Barnes & Noble "Author of the Month" for Houston and has a BA degree, combining speech communication, psychology, and art.

After writing *Where God Finds You*, Anita discovered that her favorite Bible character is the woman who touched Jesus' cloak. Anita says, "This story is very close to my heart, because of the woman's courage in the midst of terrible suffering. We really know very little about this woman, but the way she received her healing from Christ was unique and intimate and profound."

While Anita wrote *Where God Finds You*, she tried various techniques to make the biblical accounts come to life in her imagination. One way was to keep a bottle of myrrh handy. Anita says, "I think this distinctively spicy and sumptuous oil, which was used for burial purposes in biblical times, inspired me as I breathed it in and envisioned Lazarus rising from the dead."

Anita and her husband enjoy a devotional time every weekday morning in their small library. She says, "It's really a nook full of books and cozy things, including an overstuffed loveseat, but it makes for a comfortable and quiet place for us to meet with God every morning."

❧ ACKNOWLEDGMENTS ❧

Much gratitude goes to Standard Publishing editor Laura Derico, for her hard work and valuable assistance in making this manuscript the best it can be.

Appreciation goes to Bob Irvin for persuading me to write this devotional book containing biblical fiction. It was a daunting task but very fulfilling.

I also want to thank author Tosca Lee, whose brilliant and emotive work has been an inspiration to me.